HAIRLE CHONTAE

Lizzie loves

HEALTHY
FAMILY
FOOD

LIZZIE KING

HEALTHY
FAMILY
FOOD

DELICIOUS AND NUTRITIOUS MEALS YOU'LL ALL ENJOY

Lizzie ♡

For the much missed Granny Bridget, saintly Sara and Nanny

HEALTHY
FAMILY
FOOD

CONTENTS

INTRODUCTION

Coming from a large family whose focus centred on the kitchen, I've always been surrounded by incredible food and a flavour-lead, no-fuss attitude to cooking. So when I had children of my own, I wanted to instil in them a similar passion. But having scoured the range of family cookbooks available, I found that most were full of the same tired, bland nursery food, while others just didn't punch high enough in the health stakes. There seemed to be plenty of healthy cookbooks around that were aimed at adults, but where were the ones for kids and the whole family?

So I started to create my own recipes that cut out sugar and were packed full of nutritious goodies, so that my children were eating well and remained interested in food.

Inspired to learn more about the powerful effect of food on our health, I trained as a nutritional health coach and developed my skills at Leith's Cookery School. Then, in 2014, after the birth of my third child, an auto-immune disease of the thyroid (Hashimoto's) left me bed-ridden. After much trial and error, I removed gluten completely from my diet and the results were astonishing: within four months my thyroid levels had normalised and I was feeling human again.

This is the book that I desperately needed when I had my first son, nine years ago; a cookbook for kids and foodies with really delicious, super-fast, easy-to-follow recipes that are designed to be as healthy as humanly possible. A book that is densely packed with nutrient-rich foods in lip-licking flavour combinations.

I found that many of the gluten-free recipes out there were lacking in flavour and goodness and I quickly realised that other families and kids were also flummoxed by restrictive diets, and just as bound to the insipid offerings of the 'free-from' aisles at supermarkets. So I started to share my recipes online, and Lizzie Loves Healthy was born. The reaction to my blog was amazing; I started to hear from other mothers who, like me, were struggling to cook easy, healthy meals that the whole family would enjoy. Now, I'm thrilled to be sharing my absolute favourite recipes with you in this book.

I'm still amazed at the impact this way of eating has had on my family's health; my children have had ear infections and high temperatures, of course, but when stomach bugs, flu viruses and vicious colds sweep through the school, they don't fall victim.

None of them have had a sick day off school to date, which is enough for me.

All of my recipes are designed for busy mums, dads and non-parents alike; they can be made in a flash or can be left to bubble away, hands-free, so you can get on with everything else. I understand that feeding small babies and children can often be a thankless task, but with this book you won't have to cater for different tastes by slaving over three or more separate meals at a time.

I strongly believe that kids' food should not just be sub-standard alternatives to ours. Looking at the adverts on TV, you can't avoid the fizzy drinks, sugary cereals and sickly sweet bars that are being marketed to children as the norm. Kids' food should be even more health-centred than their parents', and just as exciting and delicious.

Our children are growing in brain and body at such a rapid rate, and their palates are being formed by every morsel they put in their mouths, so all the food they eat is going to affect them today and for the rest of their lives. Which is why I feel so passionately that every mouthful counts and each meal that is empty of nutritional value is an opportunity missed. We need to up our game and this book is here to help you do that.

It is crucial that we keep our children's diets broad and their taste buds awake from an early age by teaching them to enjoy healthy food. They shouldn't see it as a punishment and consider sweets a reward.

I believe that being open and honest with kids about food is the best approach. Most kids' cookbooks talk proudly about 'hiding' vegetables in recipes and using bananas or sugar to persuade them to eat something savoury, even from the very first purées and weaning foods. In my opinion, kids are less likely to enjoy their food if they don't know what's gone into it, so I aim to celebrate the ingredients that are in each of my recipes, and never to disguise them behind a veil of sweetness or purée them into unrecognisable mulch.

Flavour and goodness are most important to me, and each recipe is naturally free from gluten and refined sugars. This isn't because I'm trying to wag my finger about certain foods, but it is because I want to show that tasty, wholesome meals don't need ingredients that are at best empty of nutritional value, and at worst cause blood sugar levels to spike and suppress the immune system.

My recipes are perfect for the health conscious and for families with allergies who are bored with the 'free-from' aisles, and I hope they are also an eye opener for those who have become reliant on white flour and sweetness when cooking for children. My recipes are not vegan, vegetarian or didactic in any way. I adore a fabulous meat recipe, but vegetables are given the value they deserve. There are also lots of cakes, cookies and treats here, to demonstrate that ALL food can be full of good stuff and

enjoyed by little people too. The idea of guilt, naughtiness and virtue which is bound up in so many 'healthy' food regimes these days is categorically absent here. There is no guilt and there is no guilt-free; my food is to be enjoyed and it is designed to fuel, energise and nourish people of all ages.

I've included nuggets of nutritional information to help you choose a recipe at a glance, along with these symbols, as a shortcut to help you plan what to cook:

- VEGETARIAN (VEG)
- WEANING (W)
- BABY-LED WEANING (BLW)
- CONTAINS NUTS (N)
- CONTAINS DAIRY (D)
- VEGAN (V)

This grid of symbols appears on every recipe page to help you:

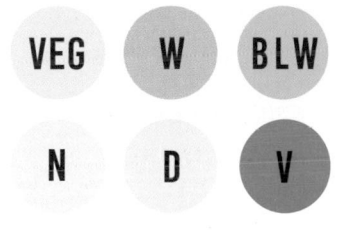

I'm fixated on time-saving as well as maximising the output of each meal, so I've highlighted when a meal can be blended as a purée for babies or mashed for toddlers, as well as when you can make something once and use part of that dish to create an even speedier dinner later in the week.

Cups are used for measuring ingredients throughout, because over the years I have found it to be the fastest, most stress-free way to cook when your hands are full. At the end of the book you'll find a variety of weekly meal plans to cover all eventualities, too, whether you need a healthy week, have no time or energy or have a special occasion to cater for.

All that remains to be said is that this book is about the joy of good, wholesome food for the whole family. It's a privilege to introduce the wonder of food to another person, and what you feed your children will be remembered forever by them. I hope you and your children share as much love and laughter while eating these dishes as I did creating them.

Lizzie x

WHAT THEY NEED WHEN & WHY

When it comes to kids, every bite counts. Their stomachs are far smaller than ours yet their calorific needs are similar: for example, a five-year-old's stomach is roughly a quarter of the size of ours, but they can need up to three-quarters of an adult's calories. Therefore everything they gobble should be packed with energy and goodness.

Every stodgy meal or fizzy drink they consume is not only hitting them with junk, but it is taking up crucial space in their tummies and leaving little room for the nutrients they actually need to stay healthy and grow to the greatest of their potential.

Always aim for a balanced diet of whole foods with plenty of fruit and vegetables. Eating the rainbow is a great way to do this: the different colours of fruits and vegetables come from the powerful phytochemicals that fight diseases. Sometimes you may need to hone in on certain nutrients at different stages of your child's development, or indeed if you notice that they may be lacking in anything – the chart on page 15 will help you do this.

WHAT A HEALTHY DIET DOES FOR A CHILD

- Promotes physical and mental growth and development

- Helps improve their concentration, brain function and learning capacity

- Ensures a healthy immune system and resistance to disease and infections

- Ensures balanced blood sugar levels and a calmer, happier disposition

- Establishes a healthy eating pattern and love of delicious food for life

* Our Children at Risk: The 5 Worst Environmental Threats to Their Health, published by the Natural Resources Defense Council (NRDC)

Top tips for getting your child on the healthy train

- Aim for choice and variety: avoid repetition and routine menus which can hinder your efforts.

- Repeat foods that are not initially popular. Children often like something after three, four or more tastes.

- Encourage new foods by using different ways of eating them – a cocktail stick with a string of fruit or veg always works for me.

- A relaxed environment always helps: try not to stand over them adding pressure, or force them to finish things.

- Involve them in shopping, choosing and chopping: this piques interest and knowledge about food and it's provenance.

- Explain basic nutritional values: knowledge excites and empowers, e.g. '**Broccoli makes your hair shiny**'. Myths and bribery don't help!

SEASONAL AND ORGANIC

I always try to eat with the seasons: it's easier, cheaper and far more nutritious when food is picked at the right time, and not forced into maturity. (Check out this website www.eattheseasons.co.uk for an easy way to stay tuned into what's best, when.)

I also think fruit and vegetables taste a whole lot better when they're fresh from the ground and haven't sat in hot lorries for days on end, so if you want to encourage young palates to love these vital foods, give them fresh ingredients that are full of flavour. A trip to a farmers' market, or strawberry picking on a beautiful summer's day are fun activities for the whole family and a great way to get kids excited about different ingredients.

I also try to buy organic when possible, as food produced this way is more nutrient-dense and free from pesticides. Children's organs are less mature than ours and they have a smaller body mass, therefore they are much more vulnerable to the chemicals contained in pesticides and their harmful effects.*

I realise that buying organic is expensive and some ingredients can be tricky to find, so you will be as relieved as I was to discover that there are certain fruits and vegetables that are not nearly as affected by pollutants, either due to the farming methods or the way the plant grows, and so can be bought without organic certification. Avocados, for example, have almost the same score when tested as organic ones, but strawberries get a high toxic

load when farmed with pesticides.
The very helpful list from The Environmental Working Group is worth having a look at. Print it off and stick on your fridge: www.ewg.org/foodnews/clean_fifteen_list.php

FOOD AS PREVENTION

Children can get very ill very quickly – temperatures soar in a matter of hours, ear drums burst – and as a parent these times are really distressing. But we can stay one step ahead by feeding them what they need, when they need it. By harnessing the nourishing power of our food, their immune systems will be at their very best, leaving them less susceptible to the many illnesses that go round schools and nurseries.

There are three things that children of all ages can do with more of, and which are worth supplementing as insurance:

- **VITAMIN D** – Mainly available from the sun, this vitamin is crucial for bone strength, immune health and general good health. Vitamin D sprays are now readily available and cheap to buy.

- **DHA EPA** (Long chain Omega 3 Fatty Acids, docosahexaenoic acid and eicosapentaenoic acid) – Oily fish is the most potent source of these essential brain-building nutrients, but hardly any of us, least of all small children, eat enough of it to satisfy our daily requirements. I recommend taking capsules or liquid forms daily.

- **PROBIOTICS** – The microbiome found in our gut is responsible for maintaining our immune system, fighting infection and processing our food. From the moment of birth, babies' guts need this good bacteria, but a constant influx of antibiotics and high-sugar foods can cause an imbalance in this system. I recommend taking probiotics regularly.

A WORD ON WATER

Water makes up more than half a child's body weight – in relative terms they need more of it than adults – and it is crucial for all bodily functions to work properly. So as children don't always recognise the signs of thirst or have as easy access to water as we do, it is crucial that we ensure that they stay hydrated.

Headaches, constipation, stomach ache and lethargy can all be signs of dehydration. On average, children need 50ml of water per kg per day – which includes water from fruits, vegetables and other sources. To help them consume this amount, I'd recommend they drink between 6 and 8 glasses of water or a liquid a day, milk included (though this needs to increase when they are ill, exercising or in a hot climate). Juices and smoothies are best drunk close to mealtimes, though, to prevent tooth decay, because of their high sugar content.

If your child turns their nose up at plain tap water, make it more appealing by adding ice cubes, lemon, lime, mint leaves, apple slices, orange segments or strawberries.

WHAT THEY NEED WHEN

To help you navigate your kids' nutritional needs as they grow, I've broken down what they need when, and how to best get these essential vitamins and minerals into their diets deliciously.

- ### AGE 0–3

Children's brains are growing incredibly fast from 0–3 years and in this time they need a higher percentage of fats in their diet. Their main initial source of calories – breast milk or formula – is made up of 50–60 per cent fat. At 6 months plus they start needing protein, because this is when their iron stores from birth have been used up, so weaning is recommended at this stage. By the age of 7 months, it is time to introduce solid foods which contain protein in some form, vegetarian or not.

- ### AGE 2–4

By the age of 2 years and up to 4, the focus is more on fibre, fruit, vegetables and whole grains, as children are better able to digest higher-fibre foods. Under 5s grow at a very fast rate, and they can do with three meals and two or three snacks a day as their energy levels increase. They can also become much fussier about food at this age – if that's your child, turn to page 16 for my 10 Steps to Cracking a Fussy Eater.

- ### AGE 5–9

The World Health Organization (WHO) estimates that a quarter of the world's population are deficient in iron, and this number is most concentrated in young children. It can be difficult to diagnose iron deficiency or anaemia without a blood test, so I suggest preempting the problem by incorporating iron-rich leafy greens, such as spinach, into meals wherever you can. This not only boosts iron levels, but children will also become more accepting of 'green bits' and should be less fussy about them in later life.

- ### AGE 10–14

The tween and teen years are when the majority of bone mass is formed, so calcium, magnesium and vitamin D are more important than ever. Girls need more iron now, too, particularly as they begin to menstruate, while boys need higher protein levels as a rule, due to their larger lean body mass.

Below is an easy-to-use chart outlining the basic calorific requirements and particular needs for each age group. As a rule, for protein requirements you can take your child's body weight and divide it by 2 – so a 100lb child would need 50g of protein.

Of course, every child is different, and gender and the time of year can change their individual requirements, so use below as a rough guide*:

	total calories	fat, protein, carbs	vitamins and minerals
12–18 months	1,000 kcals	fats, probiotics 19g fibre	DHA
18 months –3 years	1,150 kcals	fats, 20g fibre 85–100g protein	DHA
3–5 years	1,450 kcals	25g fibre 85–150g protein fruit and veg	Iron
5–8 years	1,600 kcals	25g fibre 100–170g protein	Iron
8–10 years	1,800 kcals	26g–30g fibre 140–170g protein	Iron
Over 10	1,900 kcals– 2,300kcals	28g–38g fibre 150–200g protein	Vitamin D Calcium

*Estimated average requirements for the UK

10 STEPS TO CRACKING A FUSSY EATER

Without question the most stressful part of feeding a family is dealing with picky eaters. With so many other pressures to contend with in our busy daily lives, the last thing you need is a flat refusal, plate shoving or your child spitting out food. We're programmed to nourish and feed our children, so seeing them missing meals or objecting to things can be really frustrating, and can lead us to undertake desperate measures – such as cutting out food they don't like, giving up on encouraging them to try new ingredients, and plumping for the few 'safe' meals that we know they'll eat.

While this is definitely less stressful in the short term, it only sets you and them up for a much trickier time in the long term, when they are far more likely to be fussy eaters as teenagers and adults and will miss out on the many pleasures and benefits that fabulous food can bring.

As a mother of three, I've had my fair share of dealing with this problem, and I have found that you can more easily navigate these difficult phases with a few simple techniques. Whether it's a long-term problem or a one-off tea that is being sniffed at, it is so much easier if you have a coping strategy. So say goodbye to your fussy eater and look forward to stress-free meal times!

1. PLAN FOR BEAUTIFUL VARIETY

It's so easy to fall into a routine of relying on a few family favourites, and to keep these meals on rotation. But this is where problems can creep in as children start to resist anything new. Try to introduce a new meal at least once a week. This will ensure your kids are open to new flavours and tastes, and are used to the idea of trying unknown foods. If this is tricky to start with, you can let them join in by allowing them to choose recipes from a book or a website that you like. Letting them help prepare the veg and stir the pot also engages them in their meal and may mean they're more keen to try what gets served up.

If you have the time, write up a weekly meal plan which includes these new recipes, as this keeps the stress and the last-minute panic out of meals, which is often where pressure comes from. Above all, keep changing these meal plans, as a repeated rota is limiting for both them and you.

2. REPEAT INGREDIENTS

Often it is one ingredient in particular that bears the brunt of a child's loathing, and you might find that courgettes, peppers, or something else becomes the bad guy and is sidelined at every meal. I know it can be tempting to avoid this drama by just excluding

this ingredient, but this issue can so often be nipped in the bud by employing exactly the opposite approach. I recommend keeping that ingredient in the mix but cooking it in a different way every time, and you may just find that they come round eventually. After all, their taste buds are developing all the time, and what they don't like one month might change the next.

It might also be a texture thing, so by changing it up you might find they gobble it up. When my oldest son repeatedly claimed, 'I don't like sweet potato', I used to say that foods are like people and you can't tell if you like them or not by just looking at them, you need to get to know them, as they are all different.

A roasted sweet potato, sweet potato fries, mash and sweet potato in curry are all so very different in texture, flavour and appearance. This argument really worked for me, and now my three are always prepared to try a little bit of everything before they turn their noses up at it.

3. SHOWCASE THE VEG

From the minute I became a mother I read about the tactic of 'hiding vegetables' in endless books and articles on feeding babies and children. It never felt right to me instinctively, and now, after years of cooking for endless housefuls of children, I can categorically say this is the strategy I most disagree with, because I believe it is both patronising to our children and promotes an atmosphere of distrust around food. Instead of masking ingredients, we should highlight them and make them as irresistible as possible. A good way to do this is to make the vegetable in question the delicious centre-piece of a meal, rather than a sad side which may be an afterthought for the cook and the eater.

Roasted cauliflower is a popular choice in my house, and is far more appetising than boiled florets, which can be tasteless, watery and soggy. A courgette from the oven baked in a little Parmesan or polenta is a crispy, delicious and juicy chip that is gobbled up by most kids who say they don't like them. Likewise, spiralizing a courgette into thin ribbons and serving it mixed in with pasta, is showing it off at its best.

4. GOOD, HONEST INFORMATION

As with showcasing beautiful vegetables rather than hiding them, it is important to give children real and true information about their food that will empower them, rather than patronise them with fibs. Children are savvy, and they will see right through persuasion tactics that are used to dupe them into eating things, like 'broccoli makes you a superhero'. Instead, they appreciate and respond to straightforward, honest facts.

Try out these nuggets of nutritional information at your next meal time (use more or less information depending on their age). These have worked for me time and time again:

- Spinach gives you energy to build your blood, so you can run faster in the playground.

- All the different colours in food make them great at fighting bugs, so you won't get a sore throat.

- Fish feeds your brain and makes you happier and smarter.

- Broccoli will help you make strong bones and teeth.

- Peppers will stop you getting a runny nose.

Similarly, by explaining how empty of nutrients other foods can be, rather than issuing a blanket ban on them, you are helping your child to make an informed choice that will set them up for life. After all, banning foods completely can just lead to a much-heightened desire for them and lead to binging on sweets, fizz and cakes when they're not at home. This really just delays the problem for later in life.

While children will still want to chomp on a cupcake or bag of crisps at a party, if the majority of their diet is comprised of delicious, healthy whole foods, they will taste the difference and often won't want more than a nibble as they'll find the sugar content too much for their palate. But what is crucial here is that they will have made their own choice.

5. CURB GRAZING

It's a tricky balancing act to keep children sustained throughout the day but still hungry at mealtimes, especially as they often need snacks to keep them fuelled, particularly when they are very young. However, permanently snacking on endless rice cakes, biscuits, bottles of milk, pouches of sweet fruit purée, etc, means that they will never be truly hungry, which will lead to meal refusing and then fussy eating. After all, if a child is being permanently topped up, nothing will seem that tempting, least of all something savoury and meal-shaped.

I recommend leaving at least an hour or two (depending on their ages) between a snack and the next meal. So if lunch is at 12pm and supper at 5pm, don't give them any more snacks after 10am or 3pm. And try to make these snacks easy and fast, but nutritious, such as fresh fruit, or some hummus and vegetable sticks. That way they'll be more enthusiastic about eating at their next proper meal time.

6. PARK THE EMOTIONS

It's obvious that the more stress that is felt around food and meal times, the less likely children are to want to eat well. A recent study by Erasmus MC University Medical Center in Rotterdam, Netherlands, goes further and shows that the higher levels of general stress in a household lead to much fussier eaters in the long term, too. I know that when there are temper tantrums and food is being thrown on the floor, it's easier said than done to keep your emotions in check, but by keeping calmer at meal times you will diffuse the situation and it will become a much more fun experience. So avoid repeating a mantra about

how much more they have to eat and instead try talking about something completely different, perhaps the latest book they're reading, what you're doing at the weekend, their new friend at nursery, etc.

Use aeroplanes/motorbikes/funny faces to make tiny ones find eating fun. Often distraction can be just what's needed and they'll start gobbling up what's in front of them if they don't think they're being forced. Back out of any fights at the table; if they're refusing to eat something, tell them they need to try it and then if it's still a no go, simply get on with the meal without a fuss.

Be aware that before a child gets ill – for instance if they have swollen tonsils or a sore throat – they are very likely to go off their food completely. Smoothies, soups, banana ice cream and other easily swallowed, nutrient-dense foods are what you can wheel out in these circumstances to keep their calorie intake up.

7. DO AS YOU SAY

No matter how much you talk to your kids about what's good for them, if they don't see you enjoying the foods that you offer they'll never be persuaded to eat them. If you eat well, they'll eat well. If you reach for a chocolate bar or a bag of crisps as a snack, that's what they'll want, too.

It is the tried-and-tested formula of leading by example, and double-standards will not go unnoticed.

8. INDEPENDENCE

My kids love to get involved in assembling their meals: it is more interesting than having a bowl or plate thrust upon them, and it gives them more independence, too. You can start with something familiar, like a rice bowl, and have different add-ons on the table so they can create their own bespoke supper. Try offering bowls of chopped peppers, avocado, nuts, seeds, chicken or fish, that they can just pile on to create their own rice meal mix. Build-your-own tacos or tortillas with bowls of chopped vegetables, avocados, tomatoes, cheese, sauces, etc., are great fun at the dinner table and have the added benefit of being a brilliant way to use up leftovers from the fridge.

9. TIMING

Timing is everything. If you want to try out a new dish or introduce a new ingredient into a meal but are worried about being met with resistance, pick a moment when your children's focus will be on other things, or when they've got all your attention. For example, when friends are over for a playdate your children are much less likely to make a fuss in front of them, particularly if those kids are eating up with no arguments.

Another good time to try new things is when you're not at home. If you're going on a picnic or to someone else's house, take something with you and offer it to them then. The change of environment can often be the way in. Another time when you have your kids' undivided attention and desire to please is when they are trying to avoid bedtime! I find my children are suddenly really keen to have a crunch on a new veg or taste my latest number from the stove if the alternative is going upstairs to bed!

10. KEEP IT FAMILIAR

Another winning tactic is to incorporate a particularly hated ingredient into something you know they love already. This is not the same as hiding it or masquerading it as something else, just presenting it in a different way to achieve a very different result – offer them raw spiralised courgette or roast it rather than steam it, grate cauliflower into 'rice' or roast it and serve it with a cheese sauce. So if a roast dinner or meatballs are their favourite meal, for example, try serving either one with mashed sweet potato, if that ingredient is the problem. Pancakes and patties seem to be universally liked, so use these as a vehicle for adding different ingredients: grated courgette in a fritter or sweet potato and spinach in a bhaji.

I really hope these tips are of some use to you, even if you just use a handful of them. If they only solve a couple of problems, that would make me very happy, as I am so familiar with the stress that mealtimes can induce. Please remember that perseverance is everything. Never stop trying and be confident in the knowledge that you're doing your very best for everyone.

Good Luck!

FILLING UP YOUR LARDER

Life is busier than ever; no one has the time to run to the shops every day (which can prove to be a very expensive way to live anyway), or spend hours cooking. A well-stocked cupboard will save you time and help you to keep your whole family full and healthy.

Opposite is a list of what, in an ideal world, I like to have on hand in my kitchen. These store-cupboard staples will see you through rainy Sunday afternoons, rushed midweek dinners and those evenings when you're back late and haven't had time to dash to the shops but don't want to reach for a frozen pizza.

This may look like a long list, but please don't be overwhelmed: you don't need to go out and buy it all at once. Add things in gradually and pretty soon you'll have an amazing pantry full of the healthiest of staples.

DITCH THE JUNK

Getting rid of the junk from your cupboards is just as crucial as stocking them with the good stuff. If you don't have these nasties at home, you won't be asked for them all day!

- Crisps
- Biscuits
- Sweets
- Sugary cereals

- Fizzy drinks
- Margarine
- Low-fat sugary yoghurts and drinks

- Snack bars (even the 'healthy' ones are often really high in sugar, so check the labels)

FLOURS & SUGARS

- Arrowroot
- Baking powder
- Bicarbonate of soda
- Blackstrap molasses
- Buckwheat flour
- Chestnut flour
- Coconut sugar
- Cornflour
- Gluten-free bread flour (Doves Farm do great ones)
- Gram flour
- Honey Cacao powder
- Maple syrup
- Quinoa flour
- Rice flour
- Rice syrup

SAUCES, BUTTERS & OILS

- Almond butter
- Apple cider vinegar
- Cacao butter (or dark chocolate)
- Coconut oil
- Dijon mustard
- Olive oil
- Tamari sauce

PULSES & BEANS

- Basmati rice
- Brown rice
- Chickpeas
- Green lentils
- Pasta
- Polenta
- Puy lentils
- Quinoa
- Red lentils
- Rice noodles
- Shortgrain brown rice

TINS/JARS

- Black beans
- Butter beans
- Cannellini beans
- Chickpeas
- Coconut milk
- Haricot beans
- Tinned plum tomatoes
- Tomato purée

FREEZER

- Bananas
- Berries
- Mango and pineapple
- Peas
- Spinach

NUTS, SEEDS, HERBS, SPICES & DRIED FRUIT

- Allspice
- Almonds
- Black peppercorns
- Cashews
- Cayenne
- Chia seeds
- Coriander seeds
- Cumin seeds
- Curry powder
- Dates
- Dried apricots
- Ground coriander
- Ground cinnamon or cinnamon sticks
- Ground cumin
- Linseeds
- Maldon salt
- Pecans
- Popcorn kernels
- Pumpkin seeds
- Sesame seeds
- Sunflower seeds
- Sweet smoked paprika
- Turmeric

A SUGAR-FREE FAMILY

'Sugar is 7 times more addictive than cocaine'
DR MARK HYMAN, AUTHOR OF *THE BLOOD SUGAR SOLUTION*

All the recipes in this book are made without refined sugar. People often think this is really challenging, but I want to dispel the myths, tackle the troubles and walk you through how easy it is to cook delicious foods without needing refined sugars.

WHY GO SUGAR FREE?

In simple terms, the decision to go sugar-free is about what sugar doesn't have as much as what it does have:

- It contains no essential nutrients
- Sugar decays teeth
- It affects mood, concentration and learning
- Sugar has been proven to affect long-term health
- It is highly addictive.

When you eat refined sugar (which is sugar derived from fructose and glucose), the fructose is processed then stored by the liver as glycogen if it is not needed immediately as energy. For the glucose, insulin is produced from the pancreas to use it. If you are eating sugar often and in large quantities, your liver is overloaded with glycogen which turns the fructose to fat, and this can in turn lead to Fatty Liver. So much insulin is produced that cells become 'insulin resistant', which means they no longer react as they should, and this can lead to many diseases such as obesity, type II diabetes, kidney failure, metabolic syndrome and heart disease. Scientists have shown that people who consume a lot of sugar are at a much higher risk of getting cancer*. This is believed to be because insulin is crucial for regulating uncontrolled growth and the multiplication of cells, which is exactly what cancer is. Tumour cells have 94 glucose receptors on them compared to the 4–8 on normal cells. Sugar also suppresses the immune system and is a driver of inflammation, another potential cause of cancer.

Studies conducted at Harvard have shown just how addictive sugar really is, with laboratory rats choosing refined sugar over cocaine for the dopamine 'high' that it triggers, which we are powerless to resist. Sugar hits the nucleus accumbens in the brain – the addiction centre – which is also lit up by drugs and nicotine. As dopamine is released, the dopamine receptors become dulled, exacerbating the problem and creating the addiction. So, the more we eat the more we crave, and therefore the more we need.

* 'Insulin and Cancer' by D. Boyd, published in *Integrative Cancer Therapies* (2003)

Refined sugar is high in calories and doesn't contain any other nutrients, so it provides neither us nor our children with any benefit whatsoever – it simply fills up their tiny bellies with empty calories, leaving less space for more nourishing foods. Most intrinsic sugars found in whole foods, however – such as lactose in milk and fructose in fruit etc – are bound up with water, fibre and important vitamins and minerals, thus buffering the impact of the sugar as well as providing nutritional value.

The levels of refined sugar in food and drinks today are wreaking more havoc on our children than ever before. Tooth extraction is now the single biggest reason for children under 10 being in hospital in the UK. It's almost impossible to buy any packaged foods or drinks that don't have sugar in them. Who knew how much there was added to most yoghurts, breads, sauces, fruit juices and even savoury meals and soups? That's because it's not always easy to spot on the food labels, so keep an eye out for these names often used for various sugars: brown sugar, raw sugar, cane sugar, beet sugar, turbinado, HFCS, crystallization fructose, sucrose, dextrose, glucose, lactose, maltose, Sorbitol, mannitol, malitol and xylitol.

SO, WHAT CAN WE DO ABOUT IT?
You can, of course, go 'cold turkey' and cut out sugar completely, but it's pretty tough going and not necessarily realistic. Especially given the restraints that will inevitably be inflicted on children in order to achieve this – disallowing them from joining in with friends' parties and denying them choices in restaurants. Both of which may just compound the problem.

What you can do more easily is avoid having fizzy drinks, sugary cereals, packaged cakes and biscuits in your own home, and keep the food in your cupboards as low in refined sugar as possible, so your kids don't develop much of a taste for it. Focus on what you can add into their diet instead, so it's not all about deprivation. Real, delicious whole foods are easy to make appealing and are a great way of replacing sweet treats. By ensuring all meals have a balance of good fats, protein and carbs you can balance blood sugars and will be filling your little ones up with the good stuff and leaving them not wanting for more.

Making your own snacks, cakes and treats means it's much easier to avoid sugar altogether. Homemade energy balls, smoothies and granola bars can be refined sugar-free, totally delicious and filled with goodness.

SUGAR SUBSTITUTES
Now you've ditched the white stuff, it doesn't mean you can go wild with a bottle of maple syrup – that kind of misses the point! Naturally occurring sugars/sweeteners do similar things to blood sugar levels, so our focus shouldn't be on finding a simple swap but on lowering the level of sweetness in our diet overall. Amazingly, this doesn't take long, and you'll find your taste buds soon wake up and food seems sweeter regardless. Don't believe me? Give it a week and see how sweet an apple tastes!

7 steps to sugar-free kids

1. Don't have refined sugar at home – if you don't cook with it, they won't crave it.

2. Fast-forward past the sugary food adverts on television.

3. Explain to your children what refined sugar does to them using visual cues, such as a roller coaster ride that makes them dizzy.

4. Read the labels: secret sugars hide in many unexpected things.

5. Offer an alternative such as a banana, trail mix or your own homemade treats. This is the 'crowding out' method – crowd in good foods, leaving no room for the bad.

6. Don't introduce a blanket ban – this encourages binge eating.

7. Do your main shop online or without your kids if you can – then you won't be besieged with demands for all the sugary stuff.

TOP TIP

When lowering sugar intake, a useful trick is to use these spices, vegetables and fruit in your food as natural, health-giving flavours:

- Vanilla bean
- Cacao
- Apple
- Carrot
- Berries
- Banana
- Cinnamon
- Ginger

All of these provide a lovely sweetness without any of the nasties contained in refined sugar. Use in porridge and pancakes, for example, to lessen the need for maple syrup.

NATURALLY SWEET ALTERNATIVES

Here's a brief summary of alternatives to refined sugar and what they bring to the sugar-free party:

- Maple Syrup

The pure variety is a man-made sweetener taken from the sap of the maple tree. It has mainly sucrose as its sugar make-up (the others being fructose and glucose). Sucrose is a complex sugar and is broken down into the simple sugars fructose and glucose. Beware 'maple-flavoured' syrup; this is not the real thing but a synthetic imposter and bears no relation to the true, all-natural syrup.

Verdict: Use in moderation

- Honey

Produced by bees from pollen, honey is mainly made up of fructose and glucose with a little sucrose. It contains more vitamins than maple syrup but fewer minerals. Raw, local honey is anti-microbial and anti-inflammatory because it hasn't been pasteurised.

Verdict: Use in moderation

- Agave Syrup

Contains more fructose than any other sweetener, which is way more taxing on the liver, where it is converted to glycogen and stored.

Verdict: Avoid if you can!

- Rice Malt Syrup

This is made by breaking down the starch in rice to create simple sugars. It is made up of glucose without any fructose so it isn't a burden on the liver, but it does spike blood sugar levels without providing other beneficial nutrients.

Verdict: Use in moderation

- Coconut Nectar

Made from the sap of the coconut palm tree (not to be confused with palm sugar), coconut nectar has a toffee flavour and is rich in minerals such as zinc, iron and antioxidants. Its make-up is more than 70 per cent sucrose and it is very low in fructose.

Verdict: Use in moderation

- Bananas

Loaded with potassium and fibre-rich, this is a sweet addition to food and is filled with goodness, too. Bananas provide a great boost once the kids have come in from running around outside.

Verdict: Mashed in cakes and chopped over food, bananas are a great natural sweetener. Use as needed

- Lucuma Powder

A dried fruit from the Peruvian lucuma tree, this is a naturally occurring sweetener with a caramel taste that contains many vitamins and minerals, such as iron, zinc, calcium and beta-carotene.

Verdict: Use as needed!

- Dates

Fruit of the date palm tree, dates are high in fructose but also in fibre, and they contain other vitamins and minerals, including vitamin B6, potassium and manganese. Beware that drying the fruit removes the water and concentrates the sugar, and as a result dried dates contain 30 per cent fructose.

Verdict: Use in moderation

- Blackstrap Molasses

This is made as a byproduct of sugar-cane processing and is a dark, sticky substance that isn't as sweet as other options but contains numerous minerals such as iron, calcium and manganese. It is mainly comprised of fructose and glucose.

Verdict: Use in moderation

Do be aware that all forms of sweetness – natural, unrefined or not – spike insulin levels and mean palates will crave more sweetness, so try to keep levels of all these low.

EVERYDAY
BREAKFASTS

Breakfast is so important, and for kids it's really what sets them up for the day in terms of energy. The bog-standard bowl of sugary cereal is really not doing anyone any favours. It's a blood-sugar roller coaster, leaving them crashing down by the time they get to school.

Mood, brain and body are all affected by breakfast. Studies continue to show the huge difference a filling, nutritious breakfast makes to a child's performance at school, let alone their mood. It's tough to have a cook-up in the crazy rush of a morning, so I've made sure these breakfasts are all just as easy as passing a packet of cereal. But by avoiding the sugar overload, your kids will be heads down at their desks and ready to learn.

Depending on the day of the week, there is such a difference in pace in the mornings, so I've covered a mix of instant and make-ahead breakfasts, grab-and-go ideas and slower, more decadent weekend brunches. They all pack a big punch in the nutrition stakes, and will keep little tummies full at school or at Saturday sports sessions. Some are great as puddings, snacks or lunches too, so don't feel forced into a corner; have them whenever you like.

VEG **BLW** N

BANANA BLUEBERRY BUCKWHEAT PANCAKES

| SERVES 4 |

The all-time favourite breakfast in our house, and one of the most popular recipes from my blog. Super-easy to whip up, these pancakes are fluffy with a crunch and pack tons of fruity goodness. We make them every weekend in some form or other. Sometimes everyone helps, and sometimes, for speed, I put together the dry ingredients the night before and just mix in the liquids in a flash the next morning. Buckwheat is a relative of rhubarb, and has the power of a seed rather than a grain. It's nutty, tasty, energising and nutritious; it offers so much more of everything than refined flour. It has been shown to lower cholesterol and help prevent diabetes. It contains magnesium, copper and manganese, and amazing flavonoids too, which boost the effects of the vitamin C's antioxidants.

1 cup (150g) (sprouted) buckwheat flour

½ cup (50g) ground almonds

1 tsp baking powder

½ tsp ground cinnamon

pinch sea salt

2 eggs

1 tbsp maple syrup, plus extra to drizzle

1 ripe banana, mashed well

250ml milk

2 tbsp melted butter or coconut oil

1 cup blueberries, plus extra to serve

Mix the dry ingredients in a bowl and make a well in the centre. Crack both eggs in and use a whisk to slowly combine, from the inside of the well outwards. Add the maple syrup and mashed banana, whisking slowly. Drizzle in the milk, stirring until you have a smooth, thick and pourable batter.

Melt the butter or cocount oil in a large frying pan and whisk into the batter (it will give the pancakes a glossy finish). Lastly, fold the blueberries into the batter carefully. Ladle small puddles of the batter into a hot pan, then flip when bubbles start to appear. Stack the pancakes up on a plate, drizzle with more syrup and scatter with extra fresh berries to serve.

W N V

SPICED APPLE QUINOA PORRIDGE

| SERVES 4 |

A super-tasty bowl of energy and goodness that's amazing on a chilly morning. Oats are a great energy source, full of fibre and minerals. With the addition of quinoa, this porridge packs in more protein for fuelling up. The best bit, though, is the juicy, fruity extras which are fabulous vitamin-packed flavour wonders with antibacterial goodness to beat bugs.

1 cup (90g) gluten-free oats
750ml–1 litre almond milk
sea salt, to sprinkle
1 tbsp ground cinnamon, plus
    extra to serve
2 pitted dates, finely chopped
¼ cup (40g) raisins
1 apple, cored and chopped
    or grated
1 cup quinoa flakes
1 tbsp flaked almonds
maple syrup, to drizzle

Put the oats in a pan with enough milk to cover and a sprinkle of salt. Heat gently and stir for 2–3 minutes. Stir in the cinnamon, dates, raisins and apple, and cook for 5 minutes. (Add a bit more milk if the mixture gets too dry.) Stir through the quinoa flakes and cook for another couple of minutes, continuing to add milk if needed, until thick and tender.

Divide between bowls, sprinkle with the almonds, drizzle over the maple syrup and serve with a pinch of cinnamon.

Lizzie ♥
Get your little ones to scatter over some frozen berries to cool it down, drizzle some honey on top to taste

CHOCO COCO GRANOLA

| MAKES A 500G JAR |

Some recipes come about when I'm just bored of explaining why we don't have certain foods at home, like Coco Pops. To satisfy all the Coco Pop monsters out there, make a batch of this chocolate granola. Super-easy, grain-free and packed with energy, antioxidants and minerals galore, everyone who tries it adores it. It will definitely keep you perky as a morning treat.

3 tbsp coconut oil
3 tbsp cacao powder
3 tbsp maple syrup
¼ cup (20g) flaked almonds
¼ cup (45g) buckwheat groats
½ cup coconut curls
½ cup puffed quinoa
½ cup quinoa flakes
2 tbsp sunflower seeds
2 tbsp shelled hemp seeds
1 tsp vanilla extract
pinch sea salt

Preheat the oven to 190°C/375°F/Gas mark 5. Melt the oil in a small saucepan, add the cacao powder and maple syrup and stir until smooth. Remove and set aside.

Put the almonds, buckwheat groats, coconut, puffed quinoa, quinoa flakes and seeds in a large bowl and pour over the chocolate mixture. Add the vanilla extract and salt and stir. Tip into a large baking tray and thinly spread out the mixture.

Bake for 10 minutes before turning the mixture over with a wooden spoon. Repeat at 10-minute intervals two more times, then remove from the oven when the granola is dark brown. Allow the granola to cool completely and crisp up. Keeps in an airtight jar for weeks.

Lizzie ♡ Coconut oil is high in Medium Chain Triglycerides (MCTs), healthy fats that feed the brain and lower cholesterol

VEG BLW N D

CHEESY CORNBREAD MUFFINS

| MAKES 12 MUFFINS |

The lovely yellow of the muffins and the fabulous combination of two types of corn are a winner. Perfect for tinies, weaning, parties, picnics and more. They're no-fuss and maximum taste.

1 cup (150g) cornmeal
1 cup (100g) almond flour/finely
   ground almonds
2 tbsp milled flaxseeds
2 tsp baking powder
large pinch grated nutmeg
½ tsp sea salt
3 eggs
¼ cup (60g) butter, melted
1 cup (240ml) milk of choice
½ cup grated Parmesan cheese
½ cup (90g) corn kernels (fresh,
   frozen or tinned)

KIT:
12-hole muffin tin

Tip the cornmeal, almond flour or ground almonds, flaxseeds, baking powder, nutmeg and salt into a bowl. Whisk the eggs together and combine with the butter and milk. Pour the wet ingredients into the bowl of flours and combine. Fold in the cheese and corn kernels.

Pour into a mini-muffin tin and bake for 8–10 minutes (if using a larger-size muffin tin, add 5 minutes to the cooking time).

Courgette & tomato
muffins

Cheesy cornbread
muffins

Spinach & egg
mini muffins

COURGETTE & TOMATO MUFFINS

| MAKES 12 MUFFINS |

There never seem to be enough options for filling up little lunchboxes, or for grab-and-go breakfasts straight from the freezer. These juicy bites are all that. They're super-fast, with bags of goodness. Magnesium and manganese for bone-building, and tomatoes add a powerful dose of the antioxidant lycopene. Cooking the tomatoes increases the levels of lycopene, which is a bonus.

60ml olive oil, plus 1 tbsp extra and more for greasing
1 red onion, sliced
1 cup (100g) gram (chickpea) flour
½ cup (60g) gluten-free plain flour
1 tsp baking powder
½ tsp bicarbonate of soda
½ tsp sea salt
1 egg, beaten
½ cup (120g) plain yoghurt
60ml milk
1 courgette, finely grated
4 tbsp grated Parmesan cheese (optional)
12 cherry tomatoes, each pricked once with a cocktail stick

KIT:
12-hole silicone muffin tray

Preheat the oven to 180°C/350°F/Gas mark 4. Spray the muffin tray with oil. In a small pan, heat 1 tablespoon olive oil and sweat the red onion for 5 minutes until soft. Turn off the heat.

In a mixing bowl, sift both flours, the baking powder, bicarbonate of soda and salt. Mix well. Pour in the egg, yoghurt, milk, 60ml olive oil and stir carefully with a wooden spoon until the mixture is smooth and has no remaining clumps. Try to be as light-handed as possible, as the mixture can become tough if over-mixed. Stir in the grated courgette and Parmesan cheese, if using.

Fill each muffin hole to just below the brim, then push a tomato into the top of each mound. This should mean you'll end up with pretty little chef's hat shapes as the mixture will rise over around the tomato as it bakes. Bake in the oven for 12–15 minutes until golden and puffed.

VEG BLW D

SPINACH & EGG MINI MUFFINS

| MAKES 16 MUFFINS |

These are super simple, tasty, fast and really good as an energy hit, and are perfect for little hands to gobble. They contain tons of iron and choline, which is super important for kids and mummas-to-be for healthy brain development. Eggs are also one of the only food sources of vitamin D, which we and our kids really need, especially in the colder months.

olive oil, to grease
6 eggs
50g spinach, sliced into ribbons
1 leek, finely sliced
100g grated Cheddar cheese
   or crumbled goat's cheese
sea salt and freshly ground
   black pepper

KIT:
16-hole (or two 8-hole)
   silicone mini-muffin tray
electric whisk

Preheat the oven to 180°C/350°F/Gas mark 4. Grease mini-muffin tray(s) with oil.

Crack the eggs into a bowl, season with salt and pepper and whisk with an electric whisk for a few minutes until pale and frothy. Fold in the spinach, leek and cheese, trying to keep the volume.

Pour the mixture into the mini-muffin tray. Bake for 10–15 minutes until they're golden and beautifully risen. They will droop a little while cooling. Best eaten when warm. These muffins freeze really well.

Spinach boosts iron stores and the eggs contain tryptophan which helps sleep

D

ONE-POT GREEN BAKED EGGS

| MAKES 1 POT |

A lovely, oven-baked breakfast that is pumped with dark leafy greens, these eggs are almost hands-free to make. It works really well as a cosy supper too, which looks adorable in individual ramekins. You can use any kale or greens that are in season, and the ones looking a little wilted at the back of the fridge will work just as well.

2 cubes of butter or a drizzle of
    olive oil, plus extra to grease
1 medium tomato, chopped
2 anchovy fillets in olive oil
2 cavolo nero leaves (or kale,
    spinach, spring greens),
    finely sliced
1–2 eggs
1 tbsp grated Parmesan cheese
salt and pepper

Preheat the oven to 170°C/340°F/Gas mark 3½. Butter a large ramekin. Place the chopped tomato in the bottom of the ramekin and scissor-chop the anchovies over the top. Add the finely sliced cavolo nero or greens and use the back of a spoon to press down on the leaves. Top with a couple of dots of butter or a drizzle of olive oil, and add salt and pepper to taste.

Bake in the oven for 7 minutes, until the cavolo nero looks slightly crunchy.

Crack the egg (or eggs) over the cavolo nero, and top with the Parmesan. Put back in the oven and bake for a further 12 minutes, or until the egg white is opaque but the yolk is still a little runny. Serve immediately.

VEG   N

MINI GRANOLA FRUIT CUPS

| **MAKES 24–30 MINI-MUFFINS** |

These beauties are a riff on the standard granola, although you can just bake the mix in a tray if you want to. Ideal for brunch or a party, they are really pretty little mouthfuls and always have everyone asking for more. A great gobble-on-the-go breakfast; packed with coconut, flaxseed and oats, they're an energy powerhouse with brain food to boot. The combination of cold yoghurt, juicy berries and that crunch is irresistible.

⅓ cup (70g) coconut oil

pinch flaked sea salt

¼ cup (90g) honey

3 tbsp rice syrup

1 heaped tsp ground cinnamon

1 tsp vanilla extract

1½ cup (135g) oats

½ cup (50g) quinoa flakes, or
    another ½ cup (50g) oats

2 tbsp flaxseeds

1 tbsp chia seeds

2 tbsp shredded, unsweetened
    coconut

¼ cup (40g) almond slivers

2 tbsp sesame seeds

TO SERVE
Greek yoghurt
fresh seasonal berries –
    sliced strawberries, blue-
    berries, redcurrants or
    raspberries

KIT: 24-hole mini-muffin tray

Preheat the oven to 170°C/340°F/Gas mark 3. In a small saucepan, melt the coconut oil with a pinch of salt. Add the honey, rice syrup, cinnamon and vanilla extract and stir together as it melts.

In a large bowl, combine the remaining ingredients. Pour over the coconut oil mixture and mix well. Spoon into the mini-muffin trays and use the back of a spoon to make a well in the centre. Press down firmly to form cups.

Bake for 15–20 minutes until golden. Leave to cool for a few minutes and then prise out with a knife and cool on a wire rack. These keep in an airtight container until needed (up to 3 days).

To serve, spoon dollops of Greek yoghurt into each 'cup' and top with slices of strawberries or berries of choice.

STRAWBERRY POWER PUDDING

| SERVES 4 |

This instant wonder-pot is so summery and fruity, as well as being packed with energy-giving goodness and brain power from the omega 3-rich ingredients and high-protein hit. This is decadent enough to be a pudding, virtuous enough for a healthy breakfast and has enough fuel for a midday or afternoon snack!

2 ripe bananas
60ml almond milk
2 cups (180g) strawberries,
    frozen or if fresh, hulled
seeds from 1 vanilla pod (or 1 tsp
    vanilla paste)
3 tbsp chia seeds
2 tbsp hemp seeds
1 tbsp flaxseeds

TO SERVE
1 tbsp flaked almonds
2 fresh strawberries, quarters

In a blender or food processor, whizz all the ingredients together until smooth. The pudding should still be runny at this stage, so add a dash more milk if it's very thick. Divide between 4–6 small jars, pots or ramekins and cover with cling film. Chill in the fridge for at least 1 hour and up to 24 hours.

When ready to serve, sprinkle with flaked almonds and garnish with strawberry quarters.

Lizzie
♡

High in calcium, magnesium and Omega 3 fatty acids, the chia seeds boost a dairy free diet

ROASTED ASPARAGUS & PROSCIUTTO FRITTATA

| SERVES 4 |

The perfect brunch to make ahead and have ready to slice up at the table. It's a lovely combination of textures and flavours, with green goodness as well. Asparagus is not around in the UK for long, but when it is, make this on repeat, as the taste is unbeatable. Asparagus is a great gut-health food, thanks to the prebiotic inulin. It gives a good energy boost from aspartic acid and an anti-inflammatory called rutin. Asparagus goes so perfectly with creamy fresh eggs that are rich in fats and vitamin D.

1 large bunch asparagus
2 tbsp olive oil
1 medium red onion, thinly sliced
6 eggs
5 slices prosciutto, torn into strips
4 tbsp grated Parmesan cheese
flat-leaf parsley, chopped
salt and pepper

TO SERVE
pea shoots or green leaves
1 tbsp sunflower seeds

Preheat the oven to 220°C/425°F/Gas mark 7. Line a baking tray with baking parchment. Snap the ends off the asparagus (they break where they're meant to), and toss the tips with 1 tbsp of the olive oil in a bowl. Transfer to the lined baking tray and roast in the oven for 5 minutes. Remove and set aside.

Heat the remaining olive oil in ovenproof frying pan. Add the onion and sweat gently for 5–10 minutes until translucent but not browned. Meanwhile, whisk the eggs in a bowl and season with salt and pepper. Arrange the roasted asparagus in the pan on top of the onions. Pour the eggs on top and cook over low heat for a couple of minutes. Next, lay the prosciutto slices on top, and add the Parmesan, if using. Transfer to the oven and cook for 5 minutes, until the frittata looks firm but still glossy; it will continue to cook after you take it out of the oven. I like it with a bit of give, but if you want a very firm frittata cook it for a little longer.

Serve immediately, sprinkled with chopped parsley. Serve the pea shoots as a green salad, with the sunflower seeds, on the side. Alternatively, slice up and chill in the fridge for a cold lunchbox option.

BABY SPINACH & PEA KEDGEREE

| SERVES 4 |

This kedgeree is a really hearty, filling way to start the day. Protein and greens in a breakfast bowl couldn't be better for brain-fuelling. It also works perfectly for lunches and suppers, so make a big batch and freeze portions (without the eggs) to whip out when needed.

200g cod fillets

250g undyed smoked haddock fillets

2 tbsp olive oil, plus extra to drizzle

300g brown basmati rice

2 eggs

1 onion, sliced

1 tsp turmeric

2 tsp mild curry powder

big handful of spinach (approx. 100g), shredded

1 cup frozen peas

1 tbsp chopped chives

1 tbsp chopped flat-leaf parsley

salt and pepper

Preheat the oven to 180°C/350°F/Gas mark 4. Place the fish in foil parcels with a drizzle of olive oil. Wrap tightly and place on a baking tray. Cook in the oven for about 20 minutes, until the flesh is opaque and firm to touch. Allow to cool.

Cook the rice according to the packet instructions, adding in the eggs 6 minutes before the cooking time ends to save on extra pans. Drain and remove the eggs.

Heat the 2 tablespoons of olive oil in a heavy-based saucepan, add the onion and spices along with a pinch of salt. Cook gently for 7–10 minutes, until the onion is translucent but not browned. Stir through the spinach, add the peas and allow them to heat through. Add the cooked, drained rice and stir together.

Flake the fish gently into the rice, adding the cooking juices from the foil wrappings, too.

Stir and taste for seasoning, adding more curry powder as needed and a grind or two of pepper.

Peel and quarter the boiled eggs and scatter over the top. Sprinkle with the chives and parsley and serve.

BREAKFAST BACON AVOCADO BURGER

| MAKES 4 BURGERS |

Breakfasts can often be repetitive and rushed. The rotation of muesli, granola and porridge, in our house, sometimes needs spicing up so we started giving the kids avocado and it went down a storm. Avocados are a brain-boosting, nutrient-dense gem of a breakfast food. The idea of a warm burger for breakfast is a real treat to cheer up cold, dark winter mornings. These buns are so easy to make; you can whip them up and run out the door with them if you have to. And the dough freezes really well.

FOR THE BUNS (MAKES 10)
1½ cups (225g) buckwheat flour
1 cup (120g) tapioca flour (or gluten-free flour)
1 cup porridge oats
1 tsp bicarbonate of soda
200ml plain yoghurt
100ml milk

FOR THE FILLING
8 rashers smoked streaky bacon
butter, to spread
1 avocado, sliced

Preheat the oven to 180°C/350°F/Gas mark 4. Arrange the bacon on a baking tray lined with baking paper. Cook in the oven until crisp. Line another baking tray with baking paper.

To make the buns, mix both flours, the porridge oats and bicarbonate of soda in a large mixing bowl.

In a small bowl or jug, whisk the yoghurt with the milk. Pour the wet ingredients into the dry mix and quickly combine with a knife and/or your hands, until it just comes together (don't keep kneading as this will cause the dough to become tough).

Pull off clementine-sized pieces (the dough will be very sticky at this point; that's fine) roll into a ball and place on the lined baking sheet. Bake for about 15 minutes until golden and the bottoms of the buns sound hollow when tapped.

To assemble the burgers, slice open the warm rolls, spread each with butter and place two rashers of bacon and as much avocado you can fit in before cramming the lids down.

SMOOTHIES, JUICES & ANYTHING THAT NEEDS A STRAW

All of these drinks are made in a blender, juicer or whisked together in a bottle, so they take no time at all. And they are a thousand times tastier than any shop-bought drinks. There are endless variations to play with, as seen in the Smoothie Trickle Chart opposite, which is such a handy tool for experimenting.

Drinks are one of the worst culprits when it comes to hidden, refined sugar. Even so-called 'healthy' shop-bought drinks can be an insulin-inducing disaster. My recipes, however, have lots of natural goodness from vegetables, seeds and berries. Juices are often a fibre-lacking drink that are way too sweet, but I've kept them vegetable-heavy here and just as nutrient-dense.

Kids love slurping a cold, tasty drink through a straw, which is such a great way to get them hydrated and full of vitamins effortlessly. Quite simply, it's the fastest and often cheapest way to get a boat-load of nutrients and much-needed antioxidants into tiny tummies. Particularly if children are ill, teething, sore-throated, too tired or generally off their food, a few small gulps can offer a whole heap of power and goodness.

Home-made smoothies retain their fibre, thus slowing the sugar release, and by swigging them as soon as they're made, you can be sure the vitamin and mineral content will be at its very best. Otherwise, store in the fridge for up to 24 hours.

All recipes make enough for 1 adult and 2 kids unless otherwise stated.

Lizzie ♡

They can all be poured into moulds, making for fabulous ice lollies, whatever the weather

SMOOTHIE TRICKLE CHART

Pick n' Mix! Try one from each layer and whizz up!

Liquid

Rice milk	Coconut milk	Coconut water
Almond milk	Oat milk	Rooibos chai tea

fruit

Mango	Dark cherries	Apricot/peach
Strawberries	Blueberries	Plum and apple
Banana	Raspberries	Pinapple

energy

Coconut oil	Hemp seeds	Kale
Almond butter	Avocado	Roasted sweet
Protein powder	Spinach	potato

flavour

Vanilla powder	Lucuma powder	Cacao powder
Ginger	Cinnamon	Lemon juice

extra boost

Bee pollen	Chia seeds	Maca powder
Goji and	Spirulina	Aloe
flaxseeds		

IRON-RICH ENERGY KICK

Most children under the age of ten are low in iron at some point, and as they don't routinely have blood tests it can be difficult to diagnose. Err on the side of caution and ramp up the leafy greens and root vegetables, such as beetroot, here, pumping their energy levels right up.

(V)

Ginger, Beet and Blueberry Smoothie

1 cup (160g) fresh or frozen blueberries
5cm piece fresh ginger, peeled and roughly chopped
1 tbsp chia seeds
500ml oat milk
½ beetroot, peeled and roughly chopped

Place everything in a high-speed blender and whizz until totally smooth.

(N) (V)

Hazelnut Choc Shake

500ml almond milk
2 tbsp hazelnuts
2 tbsp cacao powder, plus extra to dust
2 pitted Medjool dates
1 tbsp vanilla extract
handful of ice

Place everything in a high-speed blender and whizz until smooth. Serve with a flurry of cacao powder dusted on top.

(V)

Passion Fruit Smoothie

2 passion fruits
¼ cup (50g) cooked brown rice
500ml water
1 banana
1 tbsp flaxseeds

Place everything in a high-speed blender and whizz until totally smooth.

Lizzie ♡

If not using frozen fruit, add a handful of ice cubes to make them chilled, refreshing and more loved by littlies

Ginger, Beet
and Blueberry
Smoothie

Hazelnut Choc
Shake

Passion Fruit
Smoothie

Watermelon
Cooler

Elderflower
Cordial

Pink
Lemonade

VITAMIN C BOOSTERS

To maintain immune systems and help little people absorb iron better, it's key to keep vitamin C levels up. And these are lovely drinks to see them through summery days and hot afternoons when hydration is so crucial and water can seem boring. There's also the option to turn these into fantastic cocktails when everyone is in bed!

(V)

Watermelon Cooler

This is the fastest, tastiest, most incredible drink, which is entirely perfect for a sunny day. The lycopene present in watermelon is an amazing antioxidant – great for naturally protecting the skin from UV. Citrulline is an amino acid that helps blood flow. A mouth-watering drink to refresh and protect, how fabulous is that?

1 small watermelon, peeled
ice cubes
leaves of 2 mint sprigs

Whizz the watermelon in a high-speed blender, and add a cube or two of ice. Throw in a couple of mint leaves and whizz again. Serve with extra ice and a glug of vodka for when the kids are in bed.

(V)

Pink Lemonade

Pink lemonade is a cinch to put together, and thirst-quenchingly delicious. A perfect picnic or party number, this summery drink is one that kids adore and it's packed with goodness. Lemons have a heavy vitamin C hit, and the tasty zest is strong in antioxidants. The lemonade's antibacterial greatness will also remove toxins and boost digestion. Stir and slurp on a sunny afternoon. Zero bad guys here.

MAKES 1 LITRE
zest and juice of 2 lemons
3 tbsp maple syrup
1 litre sparkling water
1 tbsp strawberry powder (Zingology make a real strawberry one)

Stir the lemon zest, lemon juice and maple syrup together in a small jug. Decant into a wide-rim bottle along with the sparkling water. Stir, refrigerate and whip out for thirsty guzzles. ➤

(V)

Elderflower Cordial

Nothing says summer meadows quite like the smell of these white blossoms. A morning foraging for these that ends up with a long drink is always a fabulous family outing. And a draught of this cool, fragrant drink that doesn't contain kilos of sugar is a treat for everyone on a hot summer's day.

1 large bag of elderflower heads (fragrant yellow heads only)
1 vanilla pod, slit down the middle
1 whole lemon, quartered
2 litres filtered water
½ cup (140ml) honey

Remove any stems from the elderflowers, and any lurking creatures! Rinse if you need to. Place all the flowers into a large saucepan, with the vanilla pod and lemon quarters, and cover with the water. Bring to the boil, then turn the heat down and simmer, with a lid loosely covering, for 45 minutes.

Drain the hot liquid and put it back into the pan. Add the honey, then simmer on medium–high heat for 45 minutes until the liquid is reduced to 750ml at most. Leave it to cool in the pan, then use a funnel to pour into a sterilised glass bottle. Store in the fridge.

Keeps for up to a month.

(N) (V)

Plum Crumble Shake

Lots of plant-based foods, including plums, have naturally occurring antiviral properties, and nothing could be better for a small person than that.

500ml almond milk
1 cup frozen mixed plums and berries
1 pitted Medjool date
1 tbsp bee pollen
1 tbsp milled goji and flaxseeds
1 scoop vanilla protein powder (optional) for extra energy/gym goers

Place all the ingredients together in a high-speed blender and whizz until smooth.

Plum Crumble
Shake

IMMUNE BOOST

All of us need to keep our immune systems up, but kids, who are so close to each other all day, bumping into each other's snotty faces, need more of this than anyone else. As their systems are not as robust as ours, these drinks are great insurance against endless colds and infections.

(V)

Happy Green Fuel

½ large fennel bulb
large handful of spinach
2 celery stalks
½ cucumber
1 lemon, peel and pith removed
small handful of fresh basil
1 apple
1 pear
½ courgette
handful of ice, to serve
mint sprigs, to serve

Juice all ingredients and serve on ice with a sprig of mint.

(N) (V)

Tangy Tropical Oat Shake

1 banana
½ cup oats
1 tsp chia seeds
¼ cup (40g) frozen mango
1 pitted Medjool date
½ lime, peel and pith removed
2 cups (500ml) almond milk

Blend in a high-speed blender until smooth, adding more or less liquid to reach the required consistency. This one is great as a thick shake with a straw.

(V)

Coconut Cherry Burst

1 cup (250ml) coconut milk
1 cup (250ml) coconut water
1 cup (150g) frozen dark cherries
1 tsp shelled hemp seeds
desiccated coconut, to serve

Place all the ingredients together, except the desiccated coconut, in a high-speed blender and whizz until very smooth. Serve with a dusting of the desiccated coconut.

Tangy Tropical
Oat Shake

HOMEMADE MILKS

Whether or not you have issues with dairy, there are so many reasons to make a delicious nut milk to share with the family. Lactose and casein are often difficult to digest, and so prevalent in today's Western diet that to have an alternative on hand is never a bad thing. When buying nut milks, you often get barely 2% nuts, so by whizzing some up yourself in a jiffy you're adding nutrients, taste and flavour all at once.

Oat Milk

(V)

MAKES 1 LITRE
2 cups (180g) oats, soaked
    overnight in water
1 litre filtered water
pinch sea salt
dash of vanilla extract

Rinse and drain the oats. Place in a high-speed blender with the filtered water, salt and vanilla extract, and whizz until totally smooth. Strain in a sieve lined with muslin if you prefer a totally thin drink. Alternatively, use unstrained in smoothies after shaking well.

Keep in a bottle in the fridge for up to 5 days.

Rice Milk

(V)

MAKES 1 LITRE
1 cup (200g) cooked short-grain
    brown rice
1 litre filtered water
pinch sea salt
1 tsp ground cinnamon or vanilla
    extract (optional)

Tip the cooked rice into a high-powered food processor and add the water and a pinch of salt. Blend on high for a minute or so until totally smooth and liquid.

Keep in a glass bottle in the fridge for up to 5 days.

Vanilla Almond Milk

(N) (V)

MAKES 600ML
½ cup almonds, soaked
    overnight in water
600ml filtered water
pinch sea salt
1 vanilla pod
honey or maple syrup, to serve

Rinse and drain the almonds. Place in a high-speed blender with the filtered water and salt. Whizz for 3 minutes until smooth. Split the vanilla pod in half lengthways and scrape the seeds into the blender. Put the empty pod into a glass bottle. Whizz again briefly, then pour the milk into the bottle, straining through a sieve as desired. Stir through honey or maple syrup to taste and serve over ice. Store in the fridge for up to 3 days.

Vanilla
Almond Milk

Rice Milk

Oat Milk

SOUPS

The beauty of these soups is that they're all simply whizzed up in a blender, and they're packed with vegetable goodness and one of the oldest and most healing foods there is – bone broth.

Soups are great for all age groups; you can leave them chunkier for older children, or fully blend them for weaning tinies. And, at the midway stage, soup can make a lovely side for sautéed vegetables for the kids' tea, with plenty left over for supper and tomorrow's lunch. Three dishes in one, plus some extra for the freezer.

All recipes make 1.5 litres, unless otherwise stated, which is enough to serve 2 adults and 2 children.

BEST CHICKEN BONE BROTH STOCK

This is liquid gold. This bone broth stock is all the things that make me happy. It is full of flavour, provides an amazing boost to health, is almost entirely hands-free to make and couldn't be simpler or cheaper. Bubbling the bones for this long will eke out all of their possible goodness, while adding much-needed collagen – and its joint-loving and gut-healing power – to your diet. I often use this bone broth as the base for many meals, but if heated with a few vegetables or cooked meat, it can be transformed into an instant soup. Any leftover broth can be frozen in ice cube trays or portion sizes and used on days when there's nothing in the fridge. If there's one thing in this book that goes on your weekly rotation, let it be this – you'll never regret having a stash in your fridge or freezer.

1 chicken carcass, roughly
   broken up
2 celery sticks, roughly chopped
1 large carrot, chopped into
   3 or 4 pieces
1 tbsp black peppercorns
1 onion, quartered
1 tbsp apple cider vinegar
handful of parsley stalks

Place all the ingredients in a large saucepan and cover with water. Bring to the boil over a high heat, and then lower to a simmer, covering partially with a lid. Scoop off any scum that appears on the surface at the beginning and let it very gently simmer away for at least 5 hours and for up to 12 hours. Keep topping up the water every 1–2 hours.

Drain and reserve the broth in a container or fill ice cube trays, allow to cool completely then freeze. Keeps for 5 days in the fridge or 2 months in the freezer.

Pour into ice cube moulds and freeze, then store in zip lock bags for perfect-sized flavour boosts to sauces.

TANGY PRAWN ANGEL HAIR SOUP

There's always a place for more flavour but at speed, too, for hungry mouths after school, and this is a great solution. When there's a pot of stock bubbling away I love just ladling some into a next-door saucepan and creating this with just a few ingredients from the fridge and a powerhouse of taste whisked up from the cupboard. Here, you end up with a warming, fragrant and really filling bowl of goodness. The noodles are so good for twirling round chopsticks and slurping.

2 tbsp rapeseed or olive oil
2 shallots, sliced finely
1 red chilli (optional)
1 litre chicken stock (see opposite)
350g prawns, cooked or raw
¼ pointed cabbage, sliced
handful of spinach leaves,
    roughly chopped
4 chestnut mushrooms
300g vermicelli rice noodles,
    cooked according to the
    packet instructions
small bunch of coriander, torn,
    to serve

FOR THE SAUCE

1 tbsp tamari soy sauce
1 tbsp almond butter
zest and juice of 1 lime
2 tbsp sweet white miso paste
2 kaffir lime leaves, chopped
2 crushed garlic clovespaste
2.5cm crushed piece fresh
    ginger

Heat the oil in a pan and add the shallots and chilli, if using. Cook over heat for a few minutes until the shallots begin to soften.

Meanwhile, whisk together all the sauce ingredients in a small bowl.

Ladle the stock into the pan with the shallots, add the prawns and cabbage and stir for 2 minutes to heat through. Pour in the sauce and stir thoroughly, making sure everything is combined. Reduce the heat to low, add the spinach and mushrooms and cook just long enough to wilt – less than a minute.

Portion up the noodles into the bottom of the empty bowls before ladling the soup over them, then sprinkle with the torn coriander and chilli, if using.

My kids love using chopsticks with their spoons for this soup, but a word of warning: it is messy so you may need bibs!

Best Chicken
Bone Broth
Stock

Spring Ribollita
with Meatballs &
Sunflower Pistou

Tangy Prawn
Angel Hair Soup

SPRING RIBOLLITA WITH MEATBALLS & SUNFLOWER PISTOU

The perfect combo of fresh spring flavours with a bit of wintry cosiness, this soup is filling, warming and crammed with immune-kicking goodies. The pistou is a riff on your classic pesto, and consists of raw ingredients, so it is potent with antibacterial and antiviral action.

The runner beans and two types of dried beans are full of energy, vitamin C and iron – twice as much as spinach. And with antioxidants and anti-inflammatory goodness galore, this really is the best thing to get stuck into at any time of year. Traditionally, ribollita has chunks of bread stirred through to make it thicker, so do throw in some bread at the end if you want.

The meatballs are an optional add-in if you want something more substantial. You could swap them for cooked sausages instead for speed.

2 tbsp oil

1 leek, finely sliced

1 red onion, finely sliced

3 garlic cloves, finely chopped

2 carrots, diced

2 celery sticks, diced, plus 1 tbsp
chopped celery leaves

1 bay leaf

1 tsp oregano leaves

400g tin butter beans,
rinsed and drained

400g tin cannellini beans,
rinsed and drained

2 x 400g tins plum tomatoes

1 litre chicken stock (page 74)

1 cup green beans (runner
beans, French beans)

salt and pepper

FOR THE MEATBALLS

300g minced lamb

½ onion, finely chopped

2 tbsp finely chopped flat-leaf
parsley

1 tbsp oil, for frying

FOR THE PISTOU

large handful of flat-leaf parsley

3 basil sprigs

2 garlic cloves, peeled

¼ cup (35g) sunflower seeds

125ml olive oil

Heat the oil in a large casserole or saucepan over medium–low heat. Add the leek, onion and garlic and cook for 5 minutes. Reduce the heat to low, add the carrots, celery and celery leaves, bay leaf and oregano to the pan and cook for 10–15 minutes until the vegetables are really soft but not browned.

Tip in the drained beans, the tomatoes and the chicken stock, bring to the boil over high heat then turn the heat down to a low simmer and leave to bubble for 15–20 minutes, uncovered.

Meanwhile, make the meatballs. Combine all the ingredients in a large bowl and season with salt and pepper. Pluck off golf-ball-sized pieces, rolling these to form meatballs. Heat the oil in a pan, add the meatballs and brown them for a few minutes on each side. (They do not need to cook through as they will finish cooking in the soup.) Remove and set aside on a plate.

To make the pistou, put all the ingredients in a food processor and whizz to a rough green paste. Season with salt and pepper, and set aside.

When the soup has had its time, add the green beans and the browned meatballs and simmer for another 5–10 minutes until the beans are vibrant green and just softened, but not soggy. Serve with pistou spooned over.

MISO CHICKEN RICE NOODLE SOUP

My absolute favourite to bust out on a tired night, when everyone's been working hard and needs a lift more than anything. It's nourishing and cosy and is so easy to get together. With bone broth as its base and miso added in, this is a gut-healing dream for anyone who has had stomach troubles, or been on antibiotics.

1 litre chicken stock (page 74)
200g rice noodles
2 carrots
1 courgette
1 cup shredded, cooked
    chicken
2 tbsp sweet white miso paste
small handful of spinach leaves
1 red chilli (optional)
small handful of fresh coriander,
    chopped, to garnish
tamari soy sauce, to serve

Heat the stock in a saucepan and bring it to a simmer. Meanwhile, cook the rice noodles according to packet instructions.

With a potato peeler, peel ribbons off the carrots and courgette into the hot stock, letting them blanch briefly. Tip the chicken pieces into the pan. Put the miso paste in a small bowl or mug, add a ladleful of the hot stock, then mix together before pouring into the pan. Throw the spinach in just to wilt.

Add the cooked noodles and chilli, if using. Serve the soup garnished with coriander leaves and a drizzle of tamari soy sauce.

HEARTY RED LENTIL & SWEET POTATO SOUP

A multitasking winner of a soup for sure; the chopping you do now will mean so much easy deliciousness in the future. A hotpot for now, a soup tomorrow and more of both to freeze. The mighty red lentil is a saviour, as it's much lower maintenance than most legumes, pulses and beans – no soaking or boiling for hours – but it packs a mean nutritional punch. High in fibre, they keep blood sugars down, the protein fills up tummies and there's lots of magnesium, folate and iron for fuel too.

Growing children and pregnant women need lots of iron to replenish their stores for energy production. With loads of carotenoids from the vegetables, and so much goodness for your gut from the stock, this needs to be made. Swap for vegetable stock if you're vegan or vegetarian.

2 tbsp olive oil
1 onion, finely chopped
3 garlic cloves, minced
1 tsp ground cumin
1 tsp ground coriander
2 tbsp tomato purée
1 cup (190g) red lentils
1 sweet potato, peeled and diced
750ml chicken stock (page 74)
pinch of cayenne or dried chilli
    flakes (optional)
flat-leaf parsley, to garnish
few lime wedges, to squeeze
salt and pepper

Heat the oil in a large pan and gently fry the onion for 5–10 minutes. Add the garlic and spices and fry for another few minutes until fragrant. Add the tomato purée, lentils and sweet potato and turn up the heat. Pour in the stock and bring to the boil over high heat. Reduce the heat to low and simmer, covered, for 15–20 minutes, stirring occasionally, and adding boiling water if necessary. Once the lentils and sweet potato are very tender, remove the pan from the heat.

You can serve it two ways. For the kids, reserve a portion and ladle over rice as a stew. For the adults, as a soup: blend the remaining portion with a pinch of cayenne or chilli flakes and season to taste. Serve both dishes with freshly snipped parsley and a squeeze of lime.

Roast Carrot &
Coriander Soup

Hearty Red Lentil &
Sweet Potato Soup

Miso Chicken Rice
Noodle Soup

V

ROAST CARROT & CORIANDER SOUP

| MAKES 2 LITRES |

This is the cosiest bowl of goodness on an autumn day, but with so much fresh sweetness it smacks of late summer sunshine. A practically hands-free, no-chop number for busy mums, and the rest who want a satisfying meal or starter without the fuss.

1kg carrots
2 onions, roughly chopped
3 garlic cloves
1 tbsp olive oil
1 tbsp coriander seeds
1.5 litres chicken or vegetable
    stock (page 74)
handful of flat-leaf parsley,
    roughly chopped, plus extra
    to serve
1 tsp ground coriander
pumpkin seeds, to sprinkle
salt and pepper

Preheat the oven to 190°C/375°F/Gas mark 5. Chop the carrots once or twice, depending on size, to get 7cm lengths. Toss the carrots and onions in the olive oil with the garlic cloves with the seeds, and tumble into a large baking tray. Roast the veg for 30–40 minutes, turning once halfway through cooking, until soft but not fully browned. Remove from the oven and allow to cool briefly.

Tip the veg into a powerful blender along with the stock and whizz until smooth. Add the parsley and coriander and whizz again. Ladle into bowls and sprinkle with pumpkin seeds and fresh parsley. Keeps for 3 days in the fridge and freezes fabulously for up to 3 months.

PASTA, SAUCES & RICE

So often the fall-back option, pasta can be a lifesaver, but often without much flavour or goodness to go with it. These pasta meals are designed to be tasty, and fast too. The sauces will be ready to go in the same time it takes to boil the pasta.

Shop-bought bottled sauces can contain tons of sugar, lots of E numbers and plenty of unpronounceable preservatives hiding behind their benign 'organic' and 'all natural' labels.

By tweaking the classics and adding in more vegetables and flavour all round, these recipes are all jam-packed with vitamin-rich sauces that you can either make in a flash or have stashed in the freezer to whip out for a last-minute panic supper!

TUSCAN PASTA BAKE WITH CAVOLO NERO

| SERVES 4 |

It's never hard to rustle up a pasta dish, but this has the added joy of being perfect for making ahead, so it's a great crowd-feeding number. Not only does it have bags of flavour, by using quinoa pasta you're adding more goodness and protein to your bowl and the dark leafy greens pack an almighty antioxidant, calcium and iron punch. An energy-filled, immune-boosting bowl of cosy pasta is a win-win.

3 tbsp rapeseed oil

1 red onion, sliced

2 garlic cloves, minced

4 sage leaves, finely chopped

250g quinoa fusilli pasta

8 rashers of streaky bacon, chopped or 1 cup (200g) pancetta (optional)

2 × 400g tins plum tomatoes

125ml (½ cup) chicken or vegetable stock (page 74), or water

5 cavolo nero leaves, thinly sliced

3 tbsp coconut yoghurt or cream (optional)

½ cup (50g) grated Cheddar (or dairy-free) cheese

salt and pepper

Heat the oil in a large casserole dish and fry the onion, garlic and sage over medium heat for a couple of minutes. At this point, cook the pasta according to the packet instructions but take it off the heat a couple of minutes before its time is up (it will cook more in the oven). Drain well.

Turn up the heat under the casserole and add the bacon, if using. Stir and cook for about 3–4 minutes, until the bacon is browned. Add the tomatoes and stock, crushing them as you stir with the back of a wooden spoon. Bring to the boil, rinse out the tins with a splash of water and add that to the pan too. If you're not using bacon, season with salt and a big grind of black pepper. Reduce the heat to medium–low and simmer for 5 minutes until the sauce has thickened slightly. Add the cavolo nero leaves and simmer for a further 2–3 minutes.

Add the pasta to the sauce and mix really well. For a creamy version, add the coconut yoghurt or cream at this stage, and stir through. Top with the cheese. At this point, you could cover and refrigerate it until ready to cook.

Preheat the oven to 180°C/350°F/Gas mark 4. Bake for 20 minutes, until the cheese is melted and the pasta has crisp edges.

VEG W D

BUTTERNUT SQUASH & SPINACH RISOTTO

| SERVES 4 |

The bonus of a chilly night is tucking into a bowl of this creamy number which is much needed when lurgies are flying around. A family one-pot wonder: less cooking, more deliciousness! It also has some powerful bug-beating thrown in too, with lots of vitamin C and iron, as well as carotenoid antioxidants for eye health and immune boosting. As the spinach is cooked, the nutrients are more easily absorbed because the oxalic acid is broken down. And a bowl of steamed spinach is not something my kids ever eat!

2 tbsp olive oil

1 onion, thinly sliced

2 carrots, finely diced

2 celery stalks, finely diced

2 garlic cloves, crushed and chopped

300ml chicken or vegetable stock (page 74)

350g (about half) small butternut squash, in 5cm dice

300g arborio risotto rice

150ml white wine

100g spinach, finely sliced into ribbons

100g grated Parmesan cheese (mascarpone dollop optional)

handful fresh parsley, finely chopped

Heat oil in a large pan, add the onion and stir for a few minutes, adding the carrots, celery and garlic and cook gently until very soft, about 10 minutes. Add the stock to a separate saucepan and turn heat on very low, adding the butternut squash dice to cook slowly.

Turn up the heat and add the rice, stirring well to coat it and make it glossy. Pour in the wine, to sizzle. Turn down the heat and ladle some stock into the rice, leaving the squash in the stock. Stir well, and leave to simmer until more stock is required. Keep adding the stock in small amounts until the rice is cooked.

When the rice is cooked through, approximately 15 minutes depending on type, add the squash and spinach and cook for another couple of minutes.

Stir through the Parmesan, serve with parsley and a dollop of mascarpone, if you like.

SPAGHETTI VONGOLE

| SERVES 4 |

A few years ago in Italy when a local nonna made us a vongole (clam) feast and to our amazement, our then six- and four-year-olds adored the garlicky sauce and guzzled the juicy shellfish greedily. It is now a firm family favourite when in Italy and at home. Clams are an amazing source of powerful nutrients and have more iron than beef or liver. Unbelievably, six small clams provide more than a child's daily iron requirement. This dish is extremely fast and easy to make. Just get some fresh clams and have a go – your kids might adore it. Be sure to use spaghetti or linguine, as the long strands absorb the delicious briny sauce the best.

1.5kg clams
400g spaghetti or linguine
3 tbsp olive oil
4 large garlic cloves, chopped
12 cherry tomatoes, quartered
large handful of flat-leaf parsley, stalks finely chopped, leaves roughly chopped, plus extra to serve
250ml white wine
freshly ground black pepper or 1 red chilli, chopped (optional)

Put the clams in a large pan and rinse three times with cold water. Discard any opened clams and firmly tap any that aren't shut – if they then decide to close, keep them. Bring a pan of water to the boil and cook the pasta according to the packet instructions.

Pour enough olive oil in a large pan to cover the bottom and turn on the heat. About 6 minutes before the pasta is ready, add the garlic, tomatoes and parsley stalks and cook over medium–low heat, stirring, for 2–3 minutes, until the garlic starts to colour and the tomatoes start to ooze. Tumble in the clams, turn up the heat, pour in the wine, cover and cook for 5 minutes, stirring a couple of times, until all the clams are open.

Drain the pasta. Take the clams off the heat, add the pasta and parsley leaves and give it all a stir. Leave for 2 minutes so the pasta and the sauce can get it on. Put the pan in the middle of the table, scatter over some extra parsley leaves and divide between bowls. Add the chilli or pepper for those who want it. Remember to put a large bowl out for the emptied shells. The sound of them hitting it one by one as everyone races through them is the soundtrack to happiness.

FIVE-VEGETABLE BEEF RAGU

| SERVES 4 |

Everyone has a Bolognese that they rattle out, and most kids seem to love gobbling it up. It's a meaty sauce full of iron with potential for a load of vegetables to nestle in there too. There's always a stash in my freezer. This is a one-pot wonder that blips away on the stove, with a fragrant, aromatic scent that fills your house.

2 tbsp olive oil

1 onion, thinly sliced

2 carrots, finely diced

2 celery stalks, finely diced

1 courgette, diced

200g mushrooms, sliced

2 garlic cloves, chopped

2 rosemary sprigs, leaves finely
    chopped

2 thyme sprigs, leaves chopped

500g minced beef

80ml red wine

2 × 400g tins plum tomatoes

500ml chicken stock (page 74)

2 tbsp tomato purée

salt and pepper

Make a big batch and what you don't freeze you can serve again on rice with added kidney beans for a two meal, one cook wonder

Take everything out of the fridge as meat cooks much better if at room temperature and won't go chewy.

Heat the olive oil in a large, wide-based pan, add the onion and cook for a few minutes over medium–low heat until softened. Add the carrots, celery, courgette, mushrooms and garlic and cook gently for about 10 minutes until very soft.

Throw in the rosemary and thyme and stir quickly. Turn up the heat and add the minced beef, breaking up the lumps with a wooden spoon and allowing the beef to sizzle and brown for about 5 minutes. Leave the mince to brown, untouched, for another 5 minutes to allow tasty morsels to emerge at the bottom of the pan. Pour in the red wine, scraping to deglaze the pan of all those bits.

Next, add the tomatoes and 250ml of the stock and bring to the boil. Turn the heat down, partially cover the pan with the lid and leave to simmer very gently for 1½ hours. Give it a stir, add the tomato purée, seasoning and more stock if the mixture looks dry. Leave to bubble away, partially covered, for 2 hours until nicely rich and thick.

When serving with your pasta, scoop large spoonfuls into the drained pasta pan and mix together before individually plating.

VEG D

FUSILLI FLORENTINE

| SERVES 4 |

My favourite Sunday-night health hack is a speedy supper, full of greens, that tastes great. Spinach is chock-full of folate, which kids really need for red blood cells and energy, calcium for bone health and growth, and magnesium for bones, teeth and the nervous system. Eggs are omega-rich for brain boosting on a Monday morning.

300g fusilli pasta

3 eggs, plus 1 yolk, lightly whisked

handful of spinach, finely sliced into ribbons

dash of olive oil or knob of butter

freshly grated Parmesan cheese, to serve

salt and pepper

Bring a large pan of water to the boil and cook the pasta according to the packet instructions until al dente. Drain and return the pasta to the saucepan. Quickly add the eggs and egg yolk, stirring all the time over a very low heat (you don't want the heat high otherwise the eggs will scramble). Add the spinach ribbons along with a dash of olive oil or butter. Sprinkle over the Parmesan, if desired.

Lizzie ♡

The eggs are meant to be runny, but if you can't eat runny eggs do make sure you heat them through until firm

TUNA & CHERRY TOMATO PASTA

| SERVES 4 |

There are fast suppers and then there are almost-instant suppers like this. This tastes fabulous, and it is full of good things and interesting flavours that your kids might not always get to eat. My daughter discovered olives very early on and devours them, and I would never have thought to put them in her food before that.

2 tbsp olive oil

1 red onion, finely chopped

1 garlic clove, finely chopped

400g tin cherry tomatoes

2 whole thyme sprigs

60ml chicken or vegetable stock
    (page 74)

300g penne pasta

160g tin sustainably sourced
    tuna, drained

2 tbsp chopped green olives

Heat the olive oil in a large, deep-sided pan or casserole dish. Fry the onion and garlic for a few minutes until they begin to soften, then add the tomatoes, thyme and stock. Bring to the boil and leave to bubble for about 10 minutes.

Meanwhile, cook the pasta according to the packet instructions.

Gently stir the tuna and olives into the sauce. Drain the pasta, tip into the sauce and then mix well.

CREAMY COURGETTE PASTA WITH GARLIC & PUMPKIN SEED PESTO

| SERVES 4 |

A happy accident, this dish has become my new favourite thing. And it takes less time to prepare than the pasta does to cook. One pan, no washing up – genius. It's also brimming with proteins, fatty acids and green goodness from the summery courgette – a folate-full metabolic balancer with potassium and vitamin C galore.

300g fusilli pasta
1 cup (135g) cashews
zest and juice of ½ a lemon
2–3 tbsp olive oil
1 courgette, grated
basil and thyme leaves, to garnish
salt and pepper

PESTO
1 cup (130g) pumpkin seeds
1 big bunch basil, chopped
   (30g-ish)
1 tbsp chopped parsley
1 garlic clove
2 tbsp grapeseed oil
½ cup olive oil

Bring a large pan of water to the boil and cook the pasta according to the packet instructions until al dente.

Meanwhile, whizz the cashews in a food processor to get a very fine meal. Add the lemon zest and juice, then whizz. Trickle the olive oil in, with the motor running, until you have a runny paste.

To make the pesto, toast pumpkin seeds in a dry pan for 2–3 mins. Place the herbs, garlic, seeds and grapeseed oil in processor and blitz. Drizzle in the olive oil. Add water to loosen as needed.

About 2 minutes before the pasta is cooked, add the grated courgette to the pan. Once the pasta is ready, drain well. Stir in the cashew sauce, season with salt and pepper and garnish with fresh basil or thyme. Serve with a few dollops of pesto over the top.

VEGETABLES

The vibrant and infinitely diverse array of vegetables we have on offer throughout the seasons should always be at the heart of cooking. Because they taste incredible when done well, and because they are so very good for all of us.

Here, we embrace vegetables as the star of the show, or as perfect companions to roasts, as snacks or slipped into a lunchbox. No one likes a sad side of overboiled vegetable sogginess, so why would a picky toddler?

The outdated plate of meat with a couple of add-ons as a sorry excuse for vegetables has come a long way. We must celebrate everything about them, and be aware that we simply don't need to eat as much meat as all that. It's not helping us or the planet. By cooking up beautiful dishes that don't rely on a hunk of meat as the centrepiece, we are passing this crucial information on to our children too. It's their planet, and they need it to stay healthy. So here's to some unmissable planty fabulousness.

TUSCAN BAKED BEANS

| SERVES 4 |

This low-maintenance wonder blips away quietly then BINGO – it makes an incredible supper for everyone. Tuscan borlotti beans have the highest plant source of protein, not to mention are high in fibre, B vitamins and folate for DNA-making. This recipe has a couple of unexpected ingredients that really add to its depth of flavour.

3 tbsp olive oil

3 garlic cloves, sliced

1 large red onion, sliced

1 celery stalk, sliced

4–5 thyme sprigs

3 × 400g tins plum tomatoes

250ml chicken stock or
    vegetable stock (page 74)

1 cup (190g) borlotti beans,
    soaked overnight in water

1 cup (190g) haricot beans,
    soaked overnight in water

60ml blackstrap molasses

2 tbsp tomato purée

1 cup (60g) sun-blush tomatoes,
    finely chopped

baked sweet potato or crusty
    bread, to serve (optional)

Heat the olive oil in a large deep pan, add the garlic, onion, celery and thyme and sweat over a low heat for 10–15 minutes until very soft. Add the tinned tomatoes, and turn the heat up as you crush the tomatoes against the side of the pan to break them up. Bring to the boil and stir in 125ml of the stock. Reduce the heat down low and allow the sauce to bubble, partially covered, for 1 hour. Stir very occasionally to prevent sticking.

Tip both kinds of beans into the tomato sauce along with the remaining stock. Bring to the boil and then simmer gently for another 1–1½ hours until the sauce begins to thicken up. Add the molasses, tomato purée and the sun-blush tomatoes and continue to cook for another 30 minutes. Serve on a baked sweet potato or with some crusty bread, or in a bowl by itself.

BLW V

MINI PARMESAN POLENTA PIZZAS

| SERVES 4 |

An Italian staple, polenta is a fast-cook, dual-purpose wonder food. When you first cook it, it's creamy and mash-like, and you can serve it up with a meaty stew. Make double what you need and leave the remainder of it in the fridge, where it hardens. Then you can make it into lovely instant food – slice it up in rounds and fry for a tasty, crispy pizza base, or into sticks as a good ol' chip. It's ground maize, and naturally gluten free with good carotenoid content for bones, teeth and eyes. These pizza bases are topped with spinach pesto and slow-roasted tomatoes.

250ml (add more if needed) water or stock

1 pinch of sea salt

1 sprig rosemary

250g quick-cook corn-based polenta

25g butter or coconut oil

60g grated Parmesan cheese (optional)

2 tbsp olive oil

FOR THE TOPPINGS

¼ cup pesto (page 100)

½ cup (30g) sun-dried or slow-roasted tomatoes

Pour the liquid into a large, heavy-based pan along with a pinch of sea salt and a rosemary sprig, and bring to boil. Then add the polenta in a thin stream, whisking continuously. Stir for 2–3 minutes until it thickens.

Stir in the butter or oil and cheese, if using. Place the polenta in a cylindrical pot in the fridge overnight. When hardened, slice or cut out 1cm rounds and fry in a little oil in a pan for a few minutes on each side until brown and crispy.

Add pesto and tomatoes or other toppings you fancy, like cheese and ham, and crunch away.

Lizzie ♥

High in beta-carotene, polenta is great for vegetarians, and also supercharges your gut bacteria due to a special fermenting component

SMOKY THREE-BEAN & LENTIL CHILLI

| SERVES 4 |

A tweak on an old favourite that I realised my son could enjoy too at a young age. This perfect wintry supper bowl is full of cold-fighting vitamins and minerals. Serve with some fluffy brown basmati rice, or as my husband does, with lots of mashed potato.

2 tbsp olive oil
1 large red onion, finely chopped
3 garlic cloves, finely chopped
2 carrots, finely chopped
1 celery stick, finely chopped
1 red pepper, deseeded and diced
1 tsp sweet smoked paprika
½ tsp chipotle paste
3 × 400g tins plum tomatoes
200ml chicken or vegetable
    stock (page 74)
½ cup (110g) Puy lentils
400g tin red kidney beans,
    drained (or 1 cup (180g) dried,
    soaked overnight and cooked)
400g tin black beans, rinsed and
    drained (or 1 cup (180g) dried,
    soaked overnight and cooked)
400g tin pinto beans, rinsed and
    drained (or 1 cup (180g) dried,
    soaked overnight and cooked)
few coriander sprigs, stalks torn
3 tbsp tomato purée
dollop of coconut yoghurt, to
    garnish
1 red chilli, chopped (optional)
salt and pepper

Heat the olive oil in a large pan or casserole dish over a medium heat. Add the onion and garlic and fry for a couple of minutes before adding the rest of the chopped vegetables. Stir in the paprika and chipotle paste and cook for about 10 minutes, stirring every now and again until the vegetables soften.

Tip in the tomatoes and break them up a bit with the back of a wooden spoon, adding in most of the stock once you've swirled it round the emptied tomato tins to get the last of the juices out. Turn the heat up to high and bring to the boil. Once it is all bubbling, turn the heat back down to low and let it simmer gently for 45 minutes.

Add in the lentils and all the rinsed beans, with the coriander stalks, and bring to the boil. Season with salt and black pepper to taste and let it simmer gently for 30 minutes. Add the tomato purée, and another dash of stock if the chilli looks a little dry, then continue to simmer for another 30 minutes, or until the lentils and beans are tender if using soaked beans.

Divide between bowls and enjoy either as is, or with rice and a blob of yoghurt on the side. Scatter with snipped coriander leaves and chilli, if you like.

This keeps in the fridge for up to a week and freezes really well too.

15 MINS

V

QUINOA WITH MEDITERRANEAN VEGETABLES & KALE

| SERVES 4 |

This was one of the first dishes I devised especially for the weekly meals I delivered across London. Time and again I would hear from incredulous mothers that they couldn't believe their little ones had eaten quinoa, and this is the first time I've shared the magic recipe! Here, it is a great fluffy vehicle for lots of deliciously sweet Mediterranean vegetables that are at their best during the summer months. I often have this as a salad alongside some chicken or green leaves for a casual dinner or summery lunch or on a jacket potato in the winter.

200g quinoa, rinsed well

2 tbsp olive oil

2 red onions, thinly sliced

2 garlic cloves, crushed

1 red pepper, deseeded and diced

1 courgette, diced

handful of kale, finely sliced

2 tbsp tomato purée

10 basil leaves, to garnish

salt and pepper

Bring a pan of salted water to the boil and cook the quinoa for 10–15 minutes (or according to the packet instructions), until tender but not stodgy. Drain well and leave to sit in a sieve over the saucepan covered with a clean tea towel while you prepare the remaining ingredients.

Heat the olive oil in a large pan, add the onions and fry gently for a few minutes. Add the garlic, pepper and courgettes and cook, stirring, for 15 minutes, until very soft. Stir through the kale and cook until just wilted. Next, add the tomato purée and a splash of boiling water, then mix to combine. Tip the drained quinoa into the pan, season with salt and pepper and serve with a few shredded basil leaves to garnish.

Quinoa is an ancient peruvian staple, that is one of the few plant-based complete proteins, high in lysine which is key for tissue growth and repair

SWEET POTATO, COCONUT & GREEN BEAN CURRY

| SERVES 4 |

For when you need a bowlful of creamy goodness that's light and refreshing. This one is my favourite to grab from the freezer on a tired night. The coconut adds so much goodness from the lauric acid, providing antibacterial and antiviral protection for all the school lurgies and winter bugs. Ladle this up and ward off the sniffles in one go.

2 tbsp olive oil

1 onion, finely sliced

1 red onion, finely sliced

1 lemongrass stem, tough outer layer removed, trimmed and smashed

½ red chilli, sliced, plus extra to serve (optional)

small bunch coriander, stalks removed and sliced, leaves for garnish

5cm piece ginger, peeled an minced

1 tbsp mild/medium curry powder

200g tin coconut milk

400g tin plum tomatoes

2 sweet potatoes, diced

250ml chicken or vegetable stock (page 74)

100g green beans

1 tbsp cornflour (optional)

1 lime, to squeeze

Heat the olive oil in a large casserole dish or heavy based pan. Add the onions, lemongrass, chilli (if using), coriander stalks and ginger and fry gently for 5 minutes, stirring occasionally. Stir in the curry powder and cook for a further 5–10 minutes, until the onions are very soft and aromatic (don't let them brown).

Add the coconut milk, tomatoes, sweet potatoes and stock, then bring to the boil over a high heat. Reduce the heat, cover and simmer gently for 5 minutes. Add the green beans and cook for another 10 minutes, uncovered, until all the vegetables are tender but not falling apart. If the sauce is very thin, stir the cornflour with 1 tablespoon water to form a paste, add this and cook until thickened. Serve with a squeeze of lime juice, some coriander leaves and more chilli to taste, if you like.

SWEETCORN & SPINACH DHAL

| SERVES 4 |

A really cosy bowl full of so much goodness that you can rustle up from the bog-standard ingredients in your store cupboard and freezer when fresh supplies are low – after weekends and holidays especially. It's a one-pot number, too, so less washing up and barely any actual 'cooking'. Combining the lentils with rice means you're getting the full whack of essential amino acids – essential, meaning we don't make them so we need to eat them.

2 tbsp rapeseed oil

1 onion, finely sliced

2 garlic cloves, minced

½ tsp turmeric

1 tsp ground coriander

1 cup (180g) brown basmati rice
(or use white rice and halve
the cooking time)

1 litre vegetable or chicken stock
(page 74)

1 cup (180g) dried red lentils

1 cup (225g) frozen spinach

1 cup (150g) frozen sweetcorn
kernels

1 cup (225g) frozen spinach

TO SERVE

coconut yoghurt

lime wedges

coriander leaves

In a large casserole dish or heavy-based pan, heat the rapeseed oil and add the onion, garlic and spices. Stir occasionally for about 3–4 minutes until softened but not browned. Add the rice and stir through to coat in the oil and spices. Pour over 500ml of the stock and bring to the boil over a high heat. Reduce the heat to low and simmer, covered, for 30 minutes. Glance in occasionally to check the rice isn't sticking to the bottom of the pan.

Add the lentils, and a little more stock if needed. Cover and continue to simmer gently until the rice and lentils are softened, about 20 minutes. Add more stock now and again if needed. Stir in the sweetcorn and spinach and allow to blip over a low heat for a few minutes until piping hot.

Serve with a dollop of yoghurt, a squeeze of lime and a scattering of coriander leaves.

VEG BLW D

WILD MUSHROOM & DILL RISOTTO BALLS

| SERVES 4 |

This recipe gives you two meals for the price of one! The leftover risotto makes delicious bite-sized balls, perfect for canapés, kids' tea and lunchbox fillers.

1 cup (30g) dried porcini
   mushrooms
500ml chicken or vegetable
   stock (page 74)
3 tbsp olive oil
1 onion, sliced
3 garlic cloves, finely chopped
2 celery sticks, finely chopped
2 carrots, finely diced
1 tsp dried oregano
4 chestnut mushrooms, sliced
1 cup (200g) risotto rice
60ml white wine (use one you'd
   drink, it'll taste better)
100g grated Parmesan cheese
   plus optional cubes for the
   risotto balls
2 dill sprigs, chopped
salt and pepper

Tip the porcini mushrooms into a small bowl or jug, pour over hot water and leave to soak while you work. Heat the stock in a saucepan and keep it over a low heat. Heat 2 tablespoons of olive oil in a wide-based, cast-iron pan over medium-low heat. Add the onion, garlic, celery, carrots and a pinch of salt and cook for 7–10 minutes, stirring occasionally until the vegetables begin to soften. Tip in the oregano and the fresh mushrooms, and stir to combine.

Add the rice and stir to coat with the oil in the pan. Turn the heat up to high and stir for 1 minute. Then pour in the white wine. Stir well to combine, reduce the heat to medium and let the risotto bubble for a minute or two. Ladle in some of the hot stock, stir, leave to bubble until the stock has been fully absorbed, then add another ladleful. Repeat until you've used all of the stock and the water from the soaking mushrooms and the rice is slightly al dente (but not crunchy at all), about 25 minutes. Stir in the Parmesan, dill and roughly chopped soaked mushrooms. You can eat as is – risotto – for the first sitting and reserve half for making risotto balls the next day.

To make the balls, take spoonfuls of the risotto mixture and form into little balls. Sometimes I press a small square of Parmesan into the middle of each ball. Heat the remaining olive oil in a pan and fry the balls for 5–10 minutes so that they become browned and crunchy. Serve with a final scattering of Parmesan.

VEG BLW D

POLENTA TOMATO CHEESE TOASTIES

| SERVES 4 |

Polenta, an Italian wonder food, is so underused here in the UK that I always try to cook with it when possible. Made from cornmeal, naturally gluten-free and packed with carotenoid antioxidants, it's great for hair, skin and nails.

Such a versatile ingredient, it makes delicious cakes, crisp tart crusts, oven-baked fries, crunchy croutons, soft billowy mash and more. Here it is very much centre stage, replacing the slices of bread in one of my all-time childhood favourites.

1 cup (160g) polenta
4 tbsp olive oil
3 tbsp grated Parmesan cheese
2 tbsp chopped basil, plus a
    couple of leaves to serve
pinch sea salt
100g Cheddar (or other firm
    mature cheese), thinly sliced
    and cut into squares
3 tomatoes, thinly sliced
    crossways

Bring a pan of water to the boil and pour a steady stream of the polenta in, whisking all the time, until thickened, for about 3 minutes. Add half the olive oil, Parmesan and chopped basil leaves and salt and stir well.

Pour the mixture into a 25cm x 20cm baking tray lined with baking paper. You want it to be no more than 1.5cm deep. Allow to cool, then chill in the fridge to firm up for 30 minutes.

Slice the polenta into 8 or 10 lots of 3cm squares. Heat the remaining olive oil in a large pan. Add in as many polenta squares as you can fit and fry over a medium heat for about 6–8 minutes until golden brown. Flip them over carefully and cook on the other side until browned. Repeat with all of the squares. Once all sides are golden, place the slices of Cheddar on top of half the squares and allow to melt slowly for a minute or so. Top with the tomato slices and the remaining polenta squares, and serve with the basil leaves tumbled over the top.

FISH, CHICKEN & MEAT

Many of us, me included, grew up with a traditional approach to family food that featured meat front and centre – everything else had to fit in around it. As I started cooking for myself, and my own family, this focus shifted and we now have a lot of vegetable-based meals. There is still always a place for really high-quality, organic meat; just less often.

Nutritionally, both meat and fish are an extremely valuable source of protein for children, helping to build, maintain and repair the tissues in their body as well as make haemoglobin, muscles and organs, and Omega 3 fatty acids for brain development. There are important B vitamins that children can't do without, and amino acids, as well as the high levels of readily absorbed iron. I don't think any of us needs as much meat as we are used to eating, but I do firmly believe that unless a child has chosen to become vegetarian, there is a benefit from them eating animal protein of the best quality.

In this chapter, there are exciting recipes inspired by foods from all over the world. They are all here first and foremost because of how they taste. They are delicious, new and simple to make. I hope you and your children will love them.

CRISPY POLENTA-CRUSTED COD WITH SUMMER SLAW & TAHINI DRESSING

| SERVES 4 |

They are faster to make than a frozen fish finger, and are fresh and tasty beyond belief. You get all the goodness of omega fats and protein from cod, and eye- and skin-boosting minerals and carotenoids galore from the Mediterranean staple polenta. The summery crunch of the slaw is the perfect side.

300g firm white fish fillets, such
    as cod or haddock
1 cup (160g) polenta
2 tbsp rapeseed oil
lemon wedges, to serve
flat-leaf parsley, chopped
salt and pepper

FOR THE SUMMER SLAW
½ large pointed cabbage, shredded
1 large carrot, grated
1 medium courgette, grated
juice of 1 lime
1tsp sea salt
pinch dried chilli flakes (optional)
2tbsp sesame seeds

FOR THE TAHINI DRESSING
1 tsp tahini
½ tsp sesame oil
4 tbsp olive oil
1 tbsp tamari soy sauce
1 tbsp maple syrup
1 tbsp sesame seeds

Start with the slaw. Combine the vegetables with the lime juice and sea salt. Leave to wilt slightly while you make the dressing. Shake the dressing ingredients together in a jam jar and season to taste. Pour the dressing over the slaw, add the chilli flakes if using, and sprinkle with the sesame seeds. This will keep in the fridge for a day or two if making in advance.

For the fish, slice it into 5cm-long fingers. Roll the fish in the polenta, firmly patting it all over the fish pieces.

Heat the oil in a pan. Carefully drop in the fish fingers and fry for a few minutes on each side until golden and cooked through. Serve with a squeeze of lemon, a sprinkling of parsley and the tahini-dressed slaw on the side.

FLORENTINE FISHCAKES

| MAKES 15–20 FISHCAKES |

We always had fishcakes as children, and as a student I ate them a lot. There's something comforting, filling yet fresh about them, and I still love them now. With an added boost from the iron-rich spinach these are a notch above the norm. By keeping the skins on the potatoes when cooking you're preserving a huge amount of the nutrients, and saving time. Great cooked from frozen, they are perfect for when you're in a rush.

300g wild salmon fillets
250g cod fillets
250g haddock fillets
300ml milk
few flat-leaf parsley sprigs
8 black peppercorns
peeled zest of 1 lemon
700g potatoes, cut into chunks
75g butter or coconut oil, plus
    extra for frying
200g spinach leaves, finely
    sliced into ribbons
1 leek, finely sliced
1 egg, lightly beaten
salt and pepper

Place all the fish in a large pan with the milk, a sprig of parsley, peppercorns and the zest of the lemon peeled off into curls with a potato peeler. Set over a low heat and simmer, covered partially, for 10 minutes, until the fish is firm and opaque. Strain the milk into a jug, discard the seasoning and set the fish aside to cool.

Bring a large pan of salted water to the boil and cook the potatoes for 10–15 minutes until tender. Test with a fork and if they give easily, remove from the heat and drain well. Combine with the butter or coconut oil and salt and pepper, and mash until smooth. Add a splash of the poaching milk if needed – the mash should be firm and smooth, not runny.

Flake the fish into the mash, add the spinach and leek and stir. Finely chop the remaining parsley, and stir that along with the egg into the mash. Use your hands to form the mixture into small balls and flatten. Cover and chill in the fridge until needed, or freeze in ziplock bags for up to 3 months.

To cook, either bake in a preheated oven at 180°C/350°F/Gas mark 4 for 15 minutes, turning halfway through cooking, or pan-fry in a little oil, turning after a few minutes until golden.

Wild salmon is by far the best food source of Vitamin D for healthy teeth, bone growth and a boost to the immune system

SWEET MISO COD WITH WILTED CABBAGE

| SERVES 4 |

This is a super-fast spin on an Asian flavour-packed fish dish, and everyone loves it. I make mine for lunch and keep the fish marinating for the kids' supper later. Miso is a dream of a gut-healing food made from fermented soybeans; restoring probiotics and aiding digestion, it's full of protein and B vitamins and is high in antioxidants. With ginger, garlic and tons of greens, this is a great plate for bug-busting. The cabbage is a good source of vitamins A and K for strong bones.

600g cod or firm white fish fillets

4 tbsp sweet white miso

60ml tamari soy sauce, plus extra to serve

2 tbsp maple syrup

2 tbsp olive oil

5cm piece ginger, peeled and minced

2 garlic cloves, minced

1 pointed cabbage, finely sliced

1 red chilli, chopped (optional)

Cut the fish into 2.5cm cubes and place in a small bowl. Whisk together the miso, tamari, maple syrup and a splash of olive oil and pour over the fish. Stir to coat.

Heat a splash of the olive oil in a frying pan and add the ginger and garlic, stir-fry briefly on medium heat, then add the cabbage along with 2 tablespoons of water. Cover and cook for 3–5 minutes until the cabbage is just wilted.

In a small pan, heat the remaining olive oil. Add the cubes of fish, along with the marinade, and cook over medium heat for 2 minutes. Allow the fish to blacken slightly, as the miso caramelises, on each side before turning and repeating on the other side. Serve the fish over the wilted cabbage and season with more tamari to taste, and chilli, if you wish.

COCONUT-CRUSTED COD WITH MANGO SALSA

| SERVES 4 |

For those battling with getting your kids to try fish, this might be the one. The coconutty coating and the fresh, fruity salsa mean that the cod is subtly subdued, and many a fish sceptic have been turned! The coconut adds a lovely flavour and bags of good fatty acids, anti-virals and anti-fungals. Whilst the fresh fruity salsa is a vitamin rich thirst quencher.

500g cod or other firm white
    fish fillets
zest of 1 lime
1 cup (100g) unsweetened
    desiccated coconut
3 tbsp coconut flour
2 eggs, beaten

FOR THE MANGO SALSA
½ red onion, finely chopped
1 small ripe mango, peeled and
    de-stoned
1 tbsp lime juice
4 basil leaves, sliced into ribbons
1 cup (150g) cherry tomatoes,
    quartered

Soak the red onion in a small bowl of iced water while you prepare the fish.

Preheat the oven to 180°C/350°F/Gas mark 4. Slice the fish into 2.5cm-wide strips. In a bowl, combine the grated lime zest and the desiccated coconut. Put the coconut flour and eggs into two separate bowls.

Dredge the fish strips in the coconut flour, pressing it into the fish, then dip into the beaten eggs and follow with the coconut/lime zest mix.

Arrange on a baking tray lined with baking paper and bake for 20 minutes, until firm to touch and crunchy.

Meanwhile, drain the onion and assemble the ingredients for the salsa in a bowl. Then toss to combine. Serve the crunchy, coconutty fish with the salsa and a side of rice or a green salad.

PRAWN PAELLA WITH RED PEPPERS

| SERVES 4 |

I'm always trying to get more variety in to the kids' food but shellfish often gets forgotten. Prawns are a fantastic source of protein and energy, and contain high levels of zinc, crucial for children's immune systems, nervous systems and muscles. It's a filling and tasty one-pot dish you can make ahead, or mull over at the weekend.

2 tbsp olive oil

1 red onion, finely sliced

2 garlic cloves, crushed

2 celery sticks, finely chopped

5 threads saffron

¼ tsp ground turmeric

½ tsp sweet smoked paprika

1 red pepper, deseeded and sliced

250ml–500ml chicken or vegetable stock (page 74)

1 cup (195g) short-grain brown rice (or white rice if you are short of time)

250g raw shelled prawns

2 heaped tsp tomato purée

flat-leaf parsley, torn, to garnish

lemon wedges, to garnish

salt and pepper

Heat the olive oil in a large casserole dish and add the onion, garlic, celery and spices. Cook over a gentle heat for 10 minutes, stirring now and then to keep things moving and to make sure nothing browns. Season with salt and pepper to taste.

Add the sliced pepper and cook for a couple of minutes, just to soften. Pour in 250ml of the stock and add the rice. Turn up the heat and bring to the boil. Reduce the heat and simmer, covered, for about 30–40 minutes until the rice is tender. You will need to check on the paella every now and again and give it a stir to prevent sticking. Top up with the remaining stock as needed.

Finally, stir through the prawns gently so as not to break them up, add a touch more liquid and the tomato purée. Put the lid back on for 5 minutes and let it bubble gently until the prawns are opaque. Sprinkle with freshly torn parsley to serve and lemon wedges for squeezing.

PROPER FISH & CHIPS WITH TEMPURA VEGETABLES

| SERVES 4 |

We've lived next to the best fish and chip shop in London since we got married, and my kids have had plenty of George's amazing wares. So recreating the classic at home is a tough call, especially when cutting out gluten. I've tried and tried, with very mixed results, but recently I put this tempura version together and it got a thumbs up all around. The crunchy fish morsels are also delicious, and wildly popular with my kids, wrapped in corn tortillas with chopped tomatoes, lime mayonnaise and guacamole – the perfect Fish Tacos.

750g mixed potatoes and sweet
   potatoes, unpeeled, cut into
   slim wedges
3 tbsp olive oil
500g cod or other white firm
   fish fillets, cut into chunks
1 courgette, thickly sliced
1 red pepper, deseeded and cut
   into large chunks
pinch sea salt

FOR THE BATTER
100g cornflour
½ cup (60g) gluten-free flour
½ tsp ground turmeric
½ tsp baking powder
pinch sea salt
170ml sparkling water
sunflower oil, for deep-frying

Preheat the oven to 200°C/400°F/Gas mark 6. Toss the potatoes in the olive oil and salt and arrange on a large baking tray – make sure they are not piled on top of each other. Roast for about 40 minutes until golden.

Meanwhile, make the batter. In a mixing bowl, combine both flours, the turmeric, baking powder and salt. Pour in 85ml of the sparkling water and whisk to form a smooth, thick paste. Whisk in the remaining water. Pour enough safflower oil in a large saucepan to come up to 5cm, and set on a high heat.

Dip the fish pieces into the batter until nicely coated and then carefully place into the hot oil (you may need to do this in batches). Flip the fish pieces over and deep-fry for roughly 45 seconds until golden and crisp. Remove with a slotted spoon and lay on a baking tray lined with paper towels to soak up the excess oil. Place in the oven to keep warm while you continue with the remaining ingredients. Repeat the dredging and deep-frying for the rest of the fish and the vegetable pieces, and serve everything piping hot.

SALMON & FENNEL PIE

| SERVES 4 |

There's something heart-warming about the aroma of pie baking in the oven, and it's relaxingly unfussy for the cook, too. You can make this one ahead, or even in individual ramekins to keep small mouths happy. Salmon is so great for babies and children, with goodness that aids healthy brain development and boosts vitamin D levels for overall optimal performance. Like a high-quality fuel in delicious form, this pie is a treasure.

700g potatoes, cut into chunks

1 parsnip, cut into chunks

2 tbsp olive oil

2 leeks, sliced

1 fennel, very finely sliced
   (ideally use a mandoline)

1 cup (160g) frozen peas

250ml chicken stock (page 74)

3 tbsp cornflour mixed with
   2 tbsp water

350g skinless salmon fillets, cut
   into 2.5cm chunks

200g cod or other firm fish
   fillets, cut into 2.5cm chunks

3 tbsp chopped flat-leaf parsley

1 egg yolk

1 tbsp butter

salt and pepper

Preheat the oven to 180°C/350°F/Gas mark 4. Bring a large pan of salted water to the boil, add the potatoes and bring back to the boil for 5 minutes. Add the parsnip and leave to bubble for about 10 minutes until a fork goes into the potatoes and parsnip very easily. Drain well and tip back into the pan.

Meanwhile, heat the oil in a casserole dish and fry the leeks and fennel gently for 5 minutes. Add the peas, stock and cornflour mixture, and stir over a low heat for 2 minutes until it starts to thicken. Lay the fish pieces over the top and sprinkle with parsley.

Put the egg yolk and butter in the pan with the potatoes and parsnip. Mash until smooth and creamy, but don't be tempted to add any liquid – the mash needs to be firm to act as the lid on the pie. Season with salt and pepper.

Spread the mash over the fish evenly, and make fork patterns on the top. Cook in the oven for 25 minutes until piping hot and crispy at the edges.

LEMON ROAST CHICKEN WITH ORANGE & MAPLE-ROASTED ROOTS

| SERVES 4 |

Life wouldn't be the same without roast chicken. We have it once a week at least, leftover chicken being a go-to in the fridge for sandwiches and salads, or as a base for instant meals. Caramelising the lemon at the same time as roasting the chicken takes the flavours up a notch, and gives you instant gravy ready to serve straight from the pan or to pep up sauces the next day.

1 unwaxed lemon, cut lengthways and then 4 thin wedges from it

1 whole organic chicken, about 1.3 kg

2 tbsp olive oil

2 red onions, halved

salt and pepper

FOR THE ORANGE & MAPLE-ROASTED ROOTS

2 parsnips, chopped into 1cm matchstcks

4 carrots, chopped into 1cm matchstcks

2 sweet potatoes, chopped into 1cm matchsticks

4 tbsp olive oil

zest and juice of 1 orange

2 tbsp maple syrup

sea salt

Preheat the oven to 210°C/410°F/Gas mark 4. In a large baking tray, arrange the lemon pieces into a square, rinds facing out, and place the chicken on top (breast side up) so the lemons are hidden, like a little nest under the bird. Drizzle the chicken with the olive oil and sprinkle liberally with salt and pepper. Place the onions in alongside, and roast in the oven for 20 minutes.

Remove the chicken, lower the oven temperature to 150°C/300°F/Gas mark 2, and use a spoon to baste the chicken (paying particular attention to the breasts) with the juices in the pan. Return to the oven and cook for a further 50–60 minutes, depending on the size. Cooking at this lower temperature will render the meat incredibly tender, so leaving it a little longer won't hurt, but you don't want it to start drying out. Remove from the oven at the first signs of the legs looking dry. Leave to rest for 10 minutes. Toss the vegetables in the oil, orange zest and maple syrup. Spread them over one very large or two smaller baking trays and squeeze the orange juice over the top. Season with salt. Roast at 190°C/375°F/Gas mark 5 for 30–40 minutes, turning occasionally until browned. Serve slices of chicken with the juices from the lemony pan spooned over the top, alongside the vegetables.

ROAST CHICKEN & KALE STIR-FRY

| SERVES 4 |

Such a simple supper that can be made ahead, and with leftovers that can be a base for many add-ons after. It's a health kick for the whole family: brown rice is fabulous for digestion, chicken is a great source of lean protein and kale is a wonder food, as we all know, with massive amounts of calcium, iron, minerals and antioxidants for a boost to immunity and a recharge for the system.

250g short-grain brown rice

100g curly kale, tough stalks discarded and leaves sliced into fine ribbons

2 leeks, finely sliced

1 garlic clove, sliced

approx. 700g cooked roast chicken meat

2 flat-leaf parsley sprigs, chopped, to serve

Bragg Liquid Aminos, or soy sauce, for drizzling

salt and pepper

Put the rice in a pan of water with pinch of salt. Bring to the boil and simmer for as long as packet instructions require. Place the kale in a sieve or steamer attachment and cook above the rice for the final 5 minutes until wilted.

Heat a little oil in a large saucepan, add the leeks, garlic and a pinch of salt. Cook gently for 5–10 minutes, until the leeks soften and begin to brown.

Drain the rice and add to the leeks. Add the kale and stir through. Chop the chicken into bite-sized pieces and add to the rice. Sprinkle with chopped parsley, drizzle with Bragg Liquid Aminos or soy sauce.

W

SUMMER LEMON CHICKEN WITH NEW POTATOES

| SERVES 4 |

An easy one-pot zesty number that's great for the weekend – it practically cooks itself. With perfect summery flavours adding texture, pretty greens and loads of vitamins, it's packed with goodness.

60ml olive oil

1 chicken, jointed (chicken thighs, legs and breasts)

4 garlic cloves, sliced

2 onions, sliced

2 leeks, sliced

500ml chicken stock (page 74)

500g new potatoes

½ cup (80g) fresh peas

½ cup (80g) fresh broad beans (if available)

1 lemon, halved

3 mint sprigs, leaves picked

salt and pepper

Heat the oil in a large pan and brown the chicken on each side for 5–10 minutes. Turn the heat down a little, add the garlic, onions and leeks, and cook for 5 minutes, stirring, until softened.

Pour in the stock and add the new potatoes. Season with salt and pepper, and simmer gently for about 20 minutes until the chicken is cooked and the potatoes are tender.

Add the fresh peas and broad beans, if using, and leave to simmer for 3–5 minutes until softened and bright green. Squeeze over the lemon juice and stir through with the mint leaves to serve.

Lizzie ♡ Broad beans are really high in iron and copper, which keeps bones and immune systems healthy

CHICKEN & LEEK BALLS WITH CAULI-RICE

| SERVES 4 |

Tasty, full-of-flavour chicken balls that can cover so many bases. With a big energy hit they're also high on the zinc and potassium radar, essential for kids to keep their immune systems strong. Cauliflower rice is the fastest, simplest and most efficient way of getting a massive amount of this vegetable into your kids. Smothered in gluey cheese sauce or boiled within an inch of its life, cauliflower has had a rough ride until now.

FOR THE CHICKEN & LEEK BALLS

1 leek, sliced finely

1 garlic clove, minced

500g minced chicken or turkey

1 egg, beaten

50g soft butter

2 tbsp finely chopped flat-leaf parsley

3 tbsp grated Parmesan cheese

½ cup (30g) rice crumbs or breadcrumbs

oil, for frying

FOR THE CAULIFLOWER RICE

1 head cauliflower

2 tbsp olive oil

1 leek, sliced

pinch ground cumin

salt and pepper

In a mixing bowl combine the leek, garlic, mince and egg until well worked together. Take a tablespoon and scoop out some mixture, pressing into the palm of your hand to form a ball. Combine the butter with the parsley and Parmesan in a separate bowl. With a teaspoon, place a blob of mixture in the middle, then form a tightly sealed ball around this. Roll each ball firmly in the rice crumbs. Heat the oil in a pan and fry the balls for about 10 minutes, until browned all over and cooked through.

Meanwhile, make the cauliflower rice. Break the cauliflower into the bowl of a food processor and pulse-blend for 20–30 seconds until you have a rice-like consistency.

Heat the oil in a large pan, add the leek with some salt, pepper and cumin and fry for 5 minutes. Add the cauliflower and cook, stirring a couple of times, for a minute or so. Add 3–4 tablespoons of boiling water and partially cover with the lid. Cook over medium-high heat for a further 3 minutes, until there are browned edges and the vegetables are soft.

Serve the cauliflower rice with the chicken balls on the side.

WINTER MUSTARD CHICKEN

| SERVES 4 |

This was originally thought up for a class I was teaching at Daylesford Farm, but I tried it out so many times on my kids and husband that they've claimed it. It's as easy as anything, and using juicy, delicious chicken thighs that are so much cheaper than other parts always makes me happy.

6 chicken thighs

2 tbsp Dijon mustard

60ml olive oil

4 garlic cloves

2 onions, chopped

3 rosemary sprigs

2 leeks, sliced

500ml chicken stock (page 74)

2 parsnips, sliced

2 carrots, sliced

500g celeriac, chopped into chunks

handful of cavolo nero, tough stalks discarded and leaves roughly chopped

1 thyme sprig, leaves picked

salt and pepper

Smother the chicken pieces in mustard. In a large pan, heat the oil and brown the chicken on each side for 5–10 minutes. Turn the heat down a little and add the garlic, the onions, rosemary and leeks. Cook, stirring, until softened, about 5 minutes.

Pour over the stock and add the parsnips, carrots and celeriac. Season and simmer gently for about 20 minutes until the chicken is cooked and the vegetables are tender.

Add the cavolo nero and simmer for a few minutes until just wilted, stir in the thyme and serve.

Lizzie ♡ Celeriac is abundant in the colder months, with phthalides as a flavour enhancer and phosphorous for the lymphatic system

CUMIN TURKEY & SWEET POTATO PIE

| SERVES 4 |

This deliciously homely and fragrant pie came about after I had my first baby. So that we could have a Christmas drinks party with a newborn, I devised these individual festive pies perfect for everyone to eat on the hoof. They were the bomb, and I ended up making them non-stop for months. I've adapted the recipe here to make one large pie but it can easily be made in ramekins for individual portions.

2 tbsp rapeseed oil

1 large onion, chopped

3 garlic cloves, finely sliced

2 celery sticks, finely sliced

2 carrots, quartered lengthways and finely sliced

1 heaped tsp ground cumin

400g minced turkey, white and dark meat

2 tbsp tomato purée

250ml chicken or vegetable stock (page 74)

2 tbsp cornflour mixed to a paste with 2 tbsp water

coriander leaves, to garnish

FOR THE TOPPING

750g sweet potatoes

2 tbsp butter or coconut oil

Preheat the oven to 200°C/400°F/Gas mark 6. Place the sweet potatoes for the topping on the uppermost rack in the oven with a baking tray below to catch any drips. Cook for 40–60 minutes, until cooked perfectly and soft to the touch. Reduce the oven temperature to 180°C/350°F/Gas mark 4.

Heat the oil in a large casserole dish, adding the onion, garlic, celery, carrots and ground cumin, and sauté over medium heat for 7–10 minutes until softened. Turn the heat up to high and tip in the turkey mince. Move the mince around the pan as it sizzles, breaking it up with a wooden spoon, for about 3 minutes, until lightly browned.

Add the tomato purée, stock and cornflour mixture, and combine well. Bring to the boil and simmer for 2–3 minutes until slightly thickened. Turn off the heat and set aside.

To make the topping, peel the sweet potatoes and mash the flesh in a large bowl. Add the butter or coconut oil and stir until creamy. Use a spatula to smooth the mash over the turkey mixture, then fork scores on the surface in whatever pattern you like.

Bake in the oven for 20 minutes, until golden at the edges. Scatter the surface with roughly torn coriander leaves to serve.

MEXICAN PEPPER CHICKEN

| SERVES 4 |

At the beginning of the week, with leftover roast chicken on your hands, this is the fastest, tastiest supper to knock out. I always double up as it's even better the next day.

A serving of this should give a child 100% of their vitamin C for the day for an immune boost and cell growth, nearly all the vitamin A for eye health, and plenty of folate for those crucial red blood cells. Some smoky sweet paprika adds a lovely campfire flavour along with bags of nutrients, including carotenoids for eye tissue.

2 tbsp coconut/rapeseed/
olive oil

1 large onion, sliced

3 garlic cloves

½ tsp sweet smoked paprika, or
to taste

2 red peppers, deseeded and cut
into chunks

200g brown basmati rice

3 bay leaves

pinch ground cinnamon

3 × 400g tins plum tomatoes

400g cooked roast chicken
meat, torn into strips

Heat the oil in a large heavy-based pan or casserole dish, add the onion, garlic and paprika and sauté over low heat, stirring occasionally, for about 10 minutes until the onions are almost translucent and softened. Add the peppers and cook them for a couple of minutes, just to give them a chance to soften.

Cook the rice in a pan of boiling water, following the packet instructions, adding a few bay leaves and a pinch of cinnamon to the water for flavour.

Tip the tomatoes in the pan with the peppers and use the back of a wooden spoon to crush them. Bring to the boil over high heat, rinsing the tins out with 100ml water and swirling this back into the pan. Leave to bubble gently for 20–30 minutes until the sauce thickens. Throw in the cooked chicken and stir for about 5 minutes to heat through.

Drain the rice and serve bowls of it with the Mexican pepper chicken on top.

CHINESE CRISPY DUCK PANCAKES WITH HOISIN SAUCE

| SERVES 4 |

This is a clear all-time family favourite. The kids adore piling up their pancakes themselves and eating them with their fingers. And by making your own hoisin sauce in a jiffy you're adding way more fragrant flavours and none of the extra sugar of the bottled versions. Duck can be pricey but if you snap up a few when supermarkets have half-price deals, you can fill your freezer. Everyone will thank you, and it's a treat to sit down together and watch everyone assemble their own plates without having to serve up and hand round!

1 whole duck
1 tbsp olive oil
½ tsp ground cloves
salt and pepper

TO SERVE
1 cucumber
5 spring onions
2 red chillies (optional), chopped
10 Chinese rice pancakes (available from Asian supermarkets)
salt and pepper

Preheat the oven to 220°C/425°F/Gas mark 7. Trim the duck of any overhanging fleshy fat around the neck and the back. Then with a safety pin, and with your grip allowing only about 1cm spare, prick the skin all over, particularly in the folds of the thighs where it is more fatty.

Drizzle over the oil and sprinkle with ground cloves, massaging it into the duck with your fingers. Season with salt and pepper, place the duck in a baking tray and roast for 20 minutes. After this time, remove the tray from the oven and baste the duck with the juices in the tray. Reduce the oven temperature to 160°C/325°F/Gas mark 3 and roast for a further 40 minutes, basting once or twice during this time. Leave the duck to rest.

Slice the cucumber and spring onions and place in bowls for the table. We like to have a pile of chopped red chillies alongside, too. When you are ready to eat, turn the oven up to its highest setting and put the duck back in for another 10–15 minutes, until the skin is really brown and crispy. Steam the pancakes and bring to the table. Carve slices of the duck with its skin into a dish and bring to the table for everyone to assemble their pancakes.

Hoisin Sauce

1 tbsp grapeseed oil
2 garlic cloves, finely chopped
1 star anise
1 allspice
1 clove
½ cup (125ml) brown miso
¼ cup (60ml) maple syrup
1 tsp tahini
1 tbsp brown rice vinegar
1 tbsp fresh orange juice

Heat the oil in a small saucepan, add the garlic, star anise, allspice and clove, and heat gently for 2 minutes. Don't let the garlic brown.

Add in the miso paste, maple syrup, tahini, vinegar and orange juice and bring to the boil. Simmer gently for 5–10 minutes until thickened. Fish out the spice pieces and serve at room temperature.

CRISP-BAKED CHICKEN WITH ROSEMARY SWEET POTATO CHIPS & REAL KETCHUP

| SERVES 4 |

The failsafe play-date number. When you want to stick something in the oven and not think about it, but keep lots of kids happy, this one is a winner. I don't know many kids who don't love to crunch on a crispy chicken. And these wedges of sweet potato (page 159) are the perfect side with a dollop of real tomato ketchup (recipe overleaf). Shop-bought ketchup is loved by most children I know, but there is a massive amount of sugar in it so I really wanted to crack this. After much bubbling and tasting, I got this fresh, zingy delight which my kids say they prefer! Make a big batch and you'll have it for ages.

1–2 eggs

1–2 cups (120–200g) ground almonds

large pinch sweet smoked paprika

½ tsp sea salt flakes

2 heaped tbsp grated Parmesan cheese or 2 tbsp nutritional yeast (optional)

4 chicken thighs

4 chicken drumsticks

Preheat the oven to 190°C/375°F/Gas mark 5. Line a baking tray with baking parchment.

Whisk the eggs together in a bowl. In a separate bowl, combine the ground almonds with the paprika, salt and, if using, either the cheese or nutritional yeast.

Drag the chicken pieces through the egg wash, coating well all over, then press into the almond mix, making sure it's covered completely. Place on the prepared tray and cook for 30 minutes. After this time, remove the tray from the oven, turn the pieces over and reduce the oven temperature to 170°C/340°F/Gas mark 4. Return to the oven to cook for a further 15–20 minutes, until the chicken is really golden and crisp. ➤

45 MINS

BLW V

ROSEMARY SWEET POTATO WEDGES

| SERVES 4 |

2 rosemary sprigs, leaves picked
   and finely chopped
3 tbsp olive oil
1 tsp sea salt
700g sweet potato, cut into
   wedges

Preheat the oven to 190°C/375°F/Gas mark 5. Line a baking tray with baking parchment. Use a pestle and mortar to crush the rosemary with the oil and salt. Arrange the sweet potato wedges on the tray, drizzle the rosemary oil over the top, massaging well so that each piece is coated. Roast for 30 minutes, shuffle the tray to move the wedges around, and continue to cook for a further 10–15 minutes until brown and crisp on the outside.

2 HRS

V

REAL KETCHUP

| MAKES 2 LITRES |

2 tbsp olive oil
500g red onions, thinly sliced
2 celery sticks, thinly sliced
½ garlic bulb, sliced
6 allspice berries, bashed
pinch cayenne pepper
½ tsp ground cloves
1.5kg fresh tomatoes
400g tin cherry tomatoes
2 tbsp molasses
1 tbsp honey
120ml red wine vinegar

Heat the oil in a large pan. Add the onions, celery and garlic and cook over low heat until beginning to soften. Stir in the allspice, cayenne and cloves and continue to fry gently for 10 minutes. Meanwhile, put the kettle on to boil and make two shallow, skin-deep cross incisions at the base of each tomato for ease of peeling. Place the tomatoes in a small bowl, pour over enough just-boiled water to cover and leave to sit for 2 minutes. Drain and when cool enough to handle, peel them. Roughly chop the tomato flesh and add them one by one to the pan as you work.

Bring the sauce to the boil, tumble in the cherry tomatoes and simmer for 1½ hours. Tip the mixture into a blender and whizz until smooth.

CHICKEN JAMBALAYA

| SERVES 4 |

Such a cosy, warm pot that fills the house with Cajun smells galore and is full of vegetables, too, for a nutrient hit. Using a whole chicken is much cheaper and fresher than the pre-jointed pieces, and the dark meat has twice the levels of immune-boosting zinc and potassium than the white meat. Once it's all in the pot this just does its own thing and couldn't be easier. And it's really tasty. My kids love some flavour and spice, and you can just increase the chilli for the grown-ups afterwards, if needed.

2 tbsp olive oil
2 onions, finely sliced
2 celery sticks, chopped
1 tsp cayenne pepper
1 tsp sweet smoked paprika
½ tsp dried oregano
1.5kg chicken pieces (1 chicken, jointed into 6 pieces)
1 red pepper, deseeded and finely sliced
1 cup (180g) brown basmati rice
400g tin plum tomatoes
2–3 cups (500–750ml) chicken stock (page 74)
1 packed cup (100g) spinach
bunch of flat-leaf parsley, chopped, to serve
sea salt flakes and pepper

Heat the oil in a large casserole dish or heavy-based pan with a sprinkle of sea salt flakes. Add the onions, celery and spices and cook over medium-low heat for 5 minutes. Turn the heat up to high, pushing the vegetables to one side in the casserole, and sear the chicken pieces for about 3 minutes each side until browned. Remove the chicken to a plate and leave to rest.

Add the red pepper and stir for just a couple of minutes. Pour in the rice, making sure it gets a coating of the oils and spices before adding in the tomatoes and 375ml stock.

Place the chicken pieces in the casserole, ensuring everything is covered with liquid, adding more stock if needed. Bring to the boil over high heat, reduce the heat, cover tightly and simmer for 30 minutes. Check and stir occasionally, in case the liquid levels run too low and the rice sticks to the bottom. If needed, add the remaining stock, cover and simmer gently for a further 20–30 minutes until the rice is cooked. Season to taste.

Stir through the spinach, which will wilt without any extra cooking. Serve with a healthy sprinkling of chopped parsley.

W

BRAISED BEEF & WINTER VEGETABLES

| SERVES 4 |

Braised beef in a delicious sauce with so many warming root vegetables, slowly cooked to make it really tender, has been a fixture on our menu for years, loved by all ages. Beef is a great source of protein and iron, and aids absorption of many of the fat-soluble vitamins from the vegetables. Shin is a fabulous cut that melts into the sauce, and it's way cheaper, so you can go organic without breaking the bank. Parsnips, carrots, squash and more deliver a nutrient-dense punch. It's a one-pot wonder that's quick to put together and can then be left; the meltingly soft meat makes it kind on little jaws and easily mashed for tiny ones too.

3 tbsp olive oil

2 onions, sliced

4 garlic cloves

3 thyme sprigs

2 tbsp cornflour

500g shin of beef, trimmed and diced into 2.5cm pieces

4 carrots, chopped

4 parsnips, chopped

2 sweet potatoes, chopped

½ butternut squash, approx. 400g, chopped

½ small swede, approx. 400g, chopped

150ml red wine

3 × 400g tins plum tomatoes

500ml chicken stock (page 74)

2 tbsp tomato purée

salt and pepper

In a very wide, deep ovenproof pan with a lid (or casserole dish), heat the oil. Add the onions, garlic and thyme and gently fry for about 5–10 minutes, until the onions are translucent and completely softened.

Season the cornflour with salt and pepper, and then use it to dredge the beef pieces. Add the chopped vegetables to the pan and stir, over medium heat, allowing them to soften for about 5 minutes. Turn the heat up to high, add the beef and brown quickly on all sides. Pour in the wine and let it bubble for 3–4 minutes. Add the tomatoes and enough chicken stock just to cover. Bring to the boil, then turn the heat right down to a simmer. Cover almost entirely, with a tiny crack for steam to come out, and let it blip away very slowly on the lowest heat for 1½–2 hours, checking once or twice that liquid levels are not falling too drastically.

Preheat the oven to 140°C/275°F/Gas mark 1. Add the tomato purée, cover and put the pan in the oven. Cook for a further 1–2 hours, checking the liquid levels after 45 minutes and adding water or stock if necessary.

MEDITERRANEAN VEGETABLE & BACON POLENTA PIE

| SERVES 4 |

Like a quiche or a pastry pie, but made with a cornmeal crispy crust to give a lovely texture, this is a no-nonsense bake to make. It's divine served for brunch with a clean green salad on the side. Or slice it up the next day and have it cold for lunch.

FOR THE POLENTA CRUST

2 tbsp olive oil

pinch sea salt

1 cup (160g) polenta

2 tbsp grated Parmesan cheese (optional)

FOR THE FILLING

2 tbsp olive oil

1 red onion, sliced

1 red pepper, deseeded and thinly sliced

½ courgette, thinly sliced

200g rashers streaky bacon, sliced

handful of spinach leaves, roughly chopped

3 eggs

100g grated Parmesan cheese, plus extra (optional)

salt and pepper

KIT:

27cm tart tin with a removable base

To make the polenta crust, bring 600ml water to the boil in a large pan over medium heat. Add the oil and salt. In a thin, consistent stream, add the polenta, whisking all the time as it thickens. Cook until the polenta starts to blip like a volcano, about 5 minutes. Remove from the heat and whisk in the Parmesan, if using.

Preheat the oven to 180°C/350°F/Gas mark 4. Line the tart tin with baking paper to prevent any leaks. Scrape about half of the polenta into the tin and flatten it as evenly as you can until it is smooth. Make sure to work the polenta evenly up the sides. Bake in the oven for 30 minutes until the crust is golden.

Meanwhile, make the filling. In a heavy-based pan or casserole dish, heat the oil and gently sauté the onion, pepper, courgette and bacon until the vegetables are very soft and the bacon is starting to brown. Add the spinach and stir it briefly to wilt. Whisk the eggs together in a small bowl, with the cheese, if using, and some salt and pepper.

Remove the tart case from the oven and scatter the vegetable mixture evenly over the polenta. Pour over the eggs, distributing the mixture evenly in the tart. Dust with a little more Parmesan if you like. Bake in the oven for 20 more minutes until the middle is not wobbling and the surface is golden.

FRAGRANT LAMB, AUBERGINE & CHICKPEA STEW

| SERVES 4 |

Aromatic and rich, warm flavours are such a great thing to add to the menu for little people, to keep their palates awake and ready for new tastes. Lamb and aubergine in a silky sauce is a lovely way to introduce new textures and ingredients.

The intense purple of the aubergine is the plant pigment that brings a potent antioxidant called chlorogenic acid, one of the most powerful free-radical scavengers of all.

2 tbsp olive oil
1 large onion, sliced
1 carrot, diced
3 garlic cloves, minced
1 large aubergine, diced into 3cm
    cubes
1 tsp ground cumin
1 tsp ground coriander
½ tsp sweet smoked paprika
500g lamb shoulder, diced
2 × 400g tin plum tomatoes
400g tin chickpeas,
    rinsed and drained, or
    equivalent cooked
200ml chicken stock (page 74)
    or water, plus extra (optional)
salt and pepper

Preheat the oven to 180°C/350°F/Gas mark 4.

Heat the oil in a large casserole dish or heavy-based pan. Add the onion, carrot and garlic and sauté for 5 minutes. Stir in the aubergine and spices and cook for 5 minutes until softened but not brown.

Turn up the heat and add the lamb. Sear on each side quickly, turning the pieces as you go, about 3–4 minutes in total. Add the tomatoes, chickpeas and stock and season to taste. Bring to the boil, cover and put in the oven for 50 minutes–1 hour, checking the liquid levels halfway through and adding more stock or water if necessary.

CHINESE BARBECUE PORK & SPRING ONION BUNS

| MAKES ABOUT 15 BUNS |

Another one to add to the lunchbox rota, these buns are traditionally steamed, but we prefer them baked in the oven to a crunch. No longer a fluffy bun – they were never quite going to be that with the heavier, nuttier buckwheat flour – but as a crunchy bun with a juicy, meaty filling they are delicious. Cook up a stash of this fabulous barbecue sauce, and have it with anything else that is screaming out for a flavour pop.

FOR THE BARBECUE SAUCE (MAKES 150ML)

1 tsp sesame oil

2 tbsp olive oil

1 garlic, minced

¼ small Thai chilli, thinly sliced

1 shallot, finely chopped

1 tbsp finely grated ginger

2 tbsp grated carrot

2 tbsp maple syrup

100ml water or chicken stock (page 74)

2 tbsp rice wine vinegar

1 tbsp arrowroot mixed to a paste with 50ml water

salt and pepper

FOR THE BUNS

1 cup (120g) gluten-free flour, plus extra to dust

1 cup (150g) buckwheat flour

2½ tsp baking powder ➤

To make the barbecue sauce, heat both the oils, the garlic, chilli, shallot, ginger and carrot in a small saucepan. Cook, stirring, over low heat until the shallots soften. Add the remaining ingredients, including the arrowroot paste, and continue to cook for about 5 minutes, stirring over medium heat, until thickened. Leave to cool and store in a jar in the fridge if not using immediately. Keeps for up to 2 weeks.

For the buns, sift both the flours, baking powder and salt into a mixing bowl. Stir well and add the sugar. In a small cup, combine the warm water and oil. Pour this mixture into the dry ingredients, stirring to combine, but do not knead as the dough will become tough. Add a splash more water if needed to form a dough. Wrap in cling film and chill in the fridge for at least 30 minutes.

Preheat the oven to 190°C/375°F/Gas mark 5. Line a baking sheet with baking paper. To make the filling, combine all the ingredients together in a mixing bowl. Season lightly with salt and pepper.

1 tsp salt
2 tbsp coconut sugar
125ml warm water
3 tbsp olive oil

FOR THE PORK FILLING
400g minced pork
1 onion, finely chopped
1 courgette, grated
4 spring onions
1 tbsp olive oil

Heat the oil in a wok, or large frying pan, and fry the pork mixture, breaking up the chunks, until browned and completely cooked through–the pork must be completely cooked. Remove to a plate, add a few tablespoons of the barbecue sauce to taste.

Remove the dough from the fridge and divide into 3 even pieces. Then form 4 or 5 balls from each third. Using a scattering of flour on a work surface, roll out the dough (being careful as they are less robust than regular dough) into 12cm circles. Place a small teaspoon of the barbecue pork into the middle of each circle then seal by pinching to form little crinkles at the top of each bun.

Place the buns on the prepared baking sheet and cook in the oven for 12–15 minutes, until golden brown. Serve immediately, or reserve and heat through when needed.

DIJON BEEF BURGERS WITH ROSEMARY POLENTA CHIPS

| MAKES APPROX. 16 SMALL BURGERS |

Some days call for a really juicy, warming burger with some crunchy chips, but all burgers were not created equally. By opting for organic mince, you change the game on flavour, and avoid the antibiotics and hormones that do damage to kids' underdeveloped systems. These burgers are fast to put together and portions can easily be frozen to have on hand for lunchboxes, picnics and lazy days. They have lots of flavour and plenty of iron and protein for a big energy boost.

500g minced beef, preferably
    organic
1 red onion, finely chopped
4 chestnut mushrooms, finely
    chopped
2 tbsp Dijon mustard
2 tbsp olive oil, plus extra for
    frying
1 tbsp chopped thyme leaves
salt and pepper

FOR THE POLENTA CHIPS
1 cup (160g) polenta
2 tbsp olive oil, plus extra for
    frying
2 tbsp chopped rosemary
pinch sea salt

To make the polenta, bring 600ml water to the boil in a large pan over medium heat. Add the oil and salt. Add the polenta in a thin, consistent stream, whisking all the time as it thickens. Cook until the polenta starts blipping like a volcano, about 5 minutes. Remove from the heat, and stir in the rosemary.

Spread the polenta into a square baking tray (approximately 20cm x 25cm), with a depth of 2.5cm. Leave aside any excess polenta and store in the fridge for another meal. Allow to cool, then place in the fridge for 20 minutes while you make the burgers.

In a large bowl, combine the beef, onion, mushrooms, mustard, oil and thyme. Use your hands (wear disposable plastic gloves if you don't like these messy jobs) to massage and mix everything together really well, so that the meat doesn't clump and everything is uniformly combined. Season with salt and pepper and mix again.

Next, break off small fist-sized pieces and make into little patties. Leave to chill in the freezer for 5 minutes. ➤

TO SERVE

3 little gem lettuces, leaves
    pulled apart
tomatoes, sliced
cucumber, sliced
Real Ketchup (page 159)

Lizzie ♡ Quality beef is full of easily absorbed protein, iron and B vitamins, and the mustard makes it more easily digested

---

Remove the polenta from the fridge and cut them into 1cm-wide strips, about finger length. Heat a dash of oil in a frying pan and fry the polenta chips for about 5 minutes on each side, until golden brown and really crisping up. Don't be tempted to move them around before they colour because you'll want that lovely crunch. Keep warm in a low oven.

Heat a little oil in a frying pan over medium-high heat. Fry each burger for about 4 minutes on each side, depending on how thick and how well done you prefer them.

Nestle each burger into a little gem leaf and serve with a side of the crunchy polenta chips and some tomato and cucumber slices, or whatever salad or vegetables you have on hand, and dunk in the home-made ketchup on page 159.

35 MINS

D

HAM & RED PEPPER BUCKWHEAT PIZZA

| MAKES 4 SMALL PIZZAS |

Sometimes a pizza is what's required, but the frozen versions can be tasteless and lacking in goodness, and making your own dough can feel overwhelming and a headache. To the rescue one super-speedy, chock-with-health and easy-peasy buckwheat pizza crust – oh so thin and crunchy – and a topping that is made as it bakes. No time is lost and all flavour gained.

FOR THE PIZZA BASE
2 cups (300g) buckwheat flour
2 eggs
4 tbsp olive oil
2 tbsp dried oregano
1 tsp sea salt

FOR THE TOPPING
2 × 400g tins chopped
    tomatoes
2 garlic cloves, finely sliced
200g mozzarella, shredded, or
    dairy-free cheese of choice,
    grated
2 red peppers, deseeded and
    diced
200g sliced ham
salt

Preheat the oven to 200°C/400°F/Gas mark 6. In a large bowl combine the flour, eggs, olive oil, oregano and salt, mixing with a fork. Gradually pour in 2–4 tablespoons water, just enough for the mixture to come together in a ball. Divide in half and in half again to make four balls.

Roll each one out carefully on greaseproof paper, until about 25cm in diameter. Slide the paper onto a baking sheet and bake for 10 minutes.

Meanwhile, make the topping. Put the tomatoes in a saucepan with the garlic and a pinch of salt. Simmer very gently for approximately 10–15 minutes until thickened slightly.

Remove the pizza bases from the oven and spread the tomato sauce over the top of each one. Top with the mozzarella, peppers and ham. Return to the oven to bake for a further 10 minutes, until the cheese is melted and golden.

SAUSAGE, SQUASH & LENTIL HOTPOT WITH CELERIAC & PARSNIP MASH

| SERVES 4 |

Sausages and mash is that comforting staple relied upon to bring smiles to faces and fill up tummies without a mammoth effort. The iron-rich Puy lentils in this cosy hotpot and the vitmain-packed celeriac jazzing up the mash give it a nutritional upgrade from the norm, with no extra hassle or turned-up noses.

½ butternut squash

4 tbsp olive oil

1 red onion, diced

2 garlic cloves, sliced

2 celery sticks, diced

1 carrot, diced

2 cups (420g) Puy lentils

500ml chicken or vegetable stock (page 74)

1 bay leaf

8 sausages

flat-leaf parsley, chopped handful of watercress, to serve

dried chilli flakes (optional)

salt and pepper

FOR THE CELERIAC & PARSNIP MASH

1 celeriac, peeled and chopped

1 parsnip, peeled and chopped

2 tbsp olive oil

2 tbsp butter

1 heaped tbsp wholegrain mustard

Preheat the oven to 180°C/350°F/Gas mark 4. Cut the squash into 2.5cm chunks and put in a baking tray. Drizzle with 2 tablespoons oil and sprinkle with salt. Bake in oven for 20–30 minutes until tender.

Heat the remaining 2 tablespoons oil in a heavy-based pan or casserole dish. Add the onion, garlic, celery and carrot, and cook gently for 10 minutes until the vegetables start to soften. Stir in the lentils, turn up the heat to high, pour in the stock, then bring to the boil. Reduce the heat to low, add the bay leaf and simmer for 20–25 minutes, checking the liquid levels and adding more water or stock if needed. Grill the sausages in the oven for 10–15 minutes until cooked through. Add them to the lentils, along with the squash, and stir through, seasoning with salt and pepper to taste. Allow this to continue to cook while you make the mash.

To make the celeriac mash, bring a large pan of water to the boil. Add the celeriac and parsnip, and cook for 10 minutes until soft all the way through when prodded with a fork. Drain well, add the oil, butter and mustard and then mash until smooth. Season to taste. Serve the lentil hotpot atop the mash with a side of watercress and a scattering of parsley leaves. And don't forget the chilli flakes, to taste!

CORIANDER LAMB PITTA POCKETS WITH CUCUMBER PICKLE

| SERVES 4 |

Great food on the run, these nifty parcels also have a load of goodness in them. Putting together your own burgers makes them tastier, fresher and cheaper than bought ones. These are protein-rich, full of iron, brain food and bone-nourishing vitamins.

The fresh coriander is a potent anti-inflammatory, and has strong anti-histamine properties that could help hay fever sufferers. And the invisible little gems that are chia seeds are a powerhouse in nutrition; brimming with calcium for bone health and antioxidants, they do more for their weight than almost any other food.

FOR THE LAMB
500g minced lamb
1 egg, beaten
1 tbsp chia seeds
handful of coriander, chopped
1 small red onion, finely chopped
1 garlic clove, minced
salt and pepper
1 tbsp olive oil

FOR THE CUCUMBER PICKLE
1 cucumber
2 tsp rice vinegar
2 tsp coconut sugar

TO SERVE
6–8 wholemeal or gluten-free
   pitta breads, warmed
1 avocado, sliced
2 tomatoes, sliced

Make the pickle by using a vegetable peeler (or mandoline) to finely slice the cucumber. Put in a bowl and stir in the rice vinegar and the sugar. Chill in the fridge until needed.

Combine all the ingredients for the lamb in a large bowl, and season with salt and pepper. Pinch tablespoon-sized clumps of the mixture and roll into balls. Flatten onto a baking-paper lined tray and cover with cling film. Chill in the fridge until ready to cook.

Heat a little oil in a large frying pan over medium heat. Fry the patties for a couple of minutes on each side until cooked through and slide into warmed pittas with slices of avocado and tomato. If picnicking, keep separate and store in paper- or foil-lined Tupperware to insulate until you're ready to eat.

MOROCCAN-SPICED LAMB TAGINE & CAULI-COUSCOUS

| SERVES 4 |

When I first started creating recipes for other people's children, this one was by far the most popular. The sweetness of the apricots and the tenderness of the lamb all seem to go down a dream. Unsulphured apricots have loads of iron in them and the turmeric in the sauce adds in some super-powerful antioxidants, shown to halt cancer cell growth.

2 tbsp olive oil

1 onion, sliced

2 garlic cloves, sliced

1 tsp ground turmeric

1 tsp ground cumin

1 tsp ground cinnamon

2 medium carrots, diced

1 sweet potato, diced

350g trimmed lamb steaks, diced

1 cup (250ml) chicken stock (page 74)

5 dried, unsulphured apricots, roughly chopped

1 bay leaf

200g couscous

½ cauliflower

2 tbsp sultanas

1 cup (250g) coconut yoghurt

½ lime, squeezed

handful of fresh coriander, roughly chopped

handful of pomegranate seeds, to serve

Heat the oil in a large casserole dish and fry the onion and garlic gently for 2–3 minutes. Add the spices, carrots and sweet potato and heat through. Turn the heat up to high and sear the lamb pieces, turning to brown on all sides, pushing the vegetables to the edges of the pan to allow room.

Cover with stock and add in the apricots and bay leaf. Bring to the boil, turn the heat down to low and place a tightly fitting lid on to let it simmer away gently for 1 hour.

For the couscous, boil the kettle and pour over enough to cover the grains, with an extra inch. Cover and leave as per packet instructions. Blitz the cauliflower florets in the processor until rice-like. Tip into a saucepan, and over a low heat add a few tablespoons of hot water, then stir until softened a little and the water has evaporated, about 2–3 minutes. Combine with the couscous and sultanas and stir together.

In a small bowl, whisk together the yoghurt, lime juice and half of the coriander leaves. Fill bowls halfway with the cauli-couscous mix and then ladle over the lamb. Top with the yoghurt and sprinkle over remaining coriander and pomegranate jewels to finish.

SHANGHAI BEEF & PEPPER SESAME NOODLES

| SERVES 4 |

The perfect relaxed supper, this is flavour-packed and labour-light, especially if you've got a food processor to slice it all up. With five vegetables, gut-loving ginger and garlic and a protein upgrade in the buckwheat noodles, this dish is packed with energy and health.

200g buckwheat (or other) noodles
2 tbsp rapeseed oil
1 onion, finely sliced
2 garlic cloves, finely sliced
2.5cm piece ginger, peeled and finely sliced
1 large red pepper, deseeded and sliced
2 carrots, grated
1 courgette, grated
½ pointed cabbage, sliced finely
400g braising steak, trimmed and sliced
1 tbsp sesame seeds
coriander leaves, to serve
1 red chilli, sliced (optional), to serve

FOR THE SAUCE
1 tbsp tamari soy sauce
1 tbsp tahini
1 tsp sesame oil
1 tsp maple syrup
2 tbsp sesame seeds

Cook the noodles according to the instructions on the packet, drain and set aside.

Stir the sauce ingredients together in a small mug or shake up in a lidded jar, ready for adding at the end.

In a large pan, heat the oil and gently cook the onion, garlic and ginger for 5 minutes until softened. Add the remaining vegetables, turn the heat up to medium and cook for a couple of minutes. Turn the heat up high and throw in the beef, allowing it brown on each side for 1–2 minutes. The vegetables should still be slightly crunchy, so don't be tempted to keep cooking them for too long.

Add the noodles, sesame seeds and the sauce, and toss everything together thoroughly. Serve with some fresh coriander leaves and chilli for those who want it.

LUNCHBOX, PORTABLES, PICNICS & SNACKS

These are all perfect for running out the door with; whether for picnics, parties or make-ahead lunchboxes, they are delicious handfuls of goodness.

Portable foods that kids can eat with their hands are great for all stages of eating. From the early days of weaning, when some babies just want to feed themselves, to the ravenous kids after school who want to grab something and go. Not to mention being super-useful for lunches in a hurry at home.

All of the recipes here have had extra goodies added to keep the nutrient quota sky high like the Spinach Bhajis, that are such an all-time favourite from every cooking demo I've done. I hope you love these too.

SPINACH, SWEET POTATO & RED ONION BHAJIS

| MAKES 10–12 BHAJIS |

This was one of the first recipes I put up on my blog. After I posted it, everyone kept asking me to make some. They have proved to be one of my most popular creations, with adults and kids alike. And perhaps most importantly, with the chef, as they are super-easy to pull together. They are delicious served with hummus and a squeeze of lime.

2 tbsp olive oil

2 red onions, thinly sliced

1 cup (100g) gram (chickpea) flour

1 cup (155ml) water

1 large sweet potato, peeled and grated

100g spinach, finely sliced

1 tsp ground cumin

1 tsp ground turmeric

½ tsp ground coriander

salt and pepper

Heat a splash of oil in a frying pan, add the onions and fry gently for 10 minutes until softened but not browned.

In a bowl, combine the flour with the water and whisk to make a smooth batter. Add the grated sweet potato, spinach, spices, seasoning and cooked onions and stir together well.

Heat the remaining oil in a large pan and add spoonfuls of the mixture. Fry over a medium heat, until browned on both sides. Drain on some paper towel and serve immediately. Cooked bhajis can be stored in the fridge or freezer, but reheat them thoroughly before eating.

Lizzie ♡

Gram flour is naturally gluten free and high in protein, with lots of bone-building minerals like manganese, calcium and magnesium

SALMON TERIYAKI PEPPER SKEWERS

| MAKES 8 SKEWERS |

These pretty skewers are brimming with brain-boosting and bone-building goodness, making them perfect food for hungry children. So often pre-bottled sauces are mainly sugar, flavourings, gums, colours and preservatives, with nothing decent in there at all, but this teriyaki one is full of real goodness, so do make it for any number of other things besides this – in a chicken wrap, with duck or grilled fish. Once you see how easy it is to make, you'll be whipping up jars of it all the time.

400g skinless salmon, cut into
   2.5cm cubes
2 red, yellow or green peppers,
   deseeded, cut into 2.5cm
   chunks
2 tbsp oil, for frying

**FOR THE TERIYAKI SAUCE
(MAKES 75ML)**
80ml tamari soy sauce
2 tbsp mirin
2 garlic cloves, minced
2.5cm piece ginger, peeled and
   minced
2 tbsp maple syrup
1 tsp sesame oil
1 tbsp cornflour

KIT:
8 bamboo skewers, soaked in
   water

Start with the sauce. Place the tamari, mirin, garlic, ginger and 1 tablespoon water into a small saucepan and heat gently until simmering. Add the maple syrup and sesame oil, and let it bubble very gently over low heat for 5 minutes for all the flavours to infuse.

In a small cup, stir together the cornflour and 1 tablespoon water to a smooth paste, and whisk this into the pan. Cook for 2 minutes, continuing to whisk as the sauce thickens. Remove from the heat and set aside.

Thread the salmon and peppers onto the soaked bamboo skewers alternately, about four or five of each. Paint a thin layer of the sauce over each of the skewers, leaving the majority in the pan for later. In a large frying pan or griddle pan, heat the oil and sear the skewers on all sides for a couple of minutes. You can leave them at this stage until needed. When ready to serve, arrange the skewers on a baking sheet and finish cooking in an oven preheated to 180°C/350°F/Gas mark 4 for 10 minutes.

Serve with fluffy rice, quinoa or couscous and slather on as much teriyaki sauce as you like.

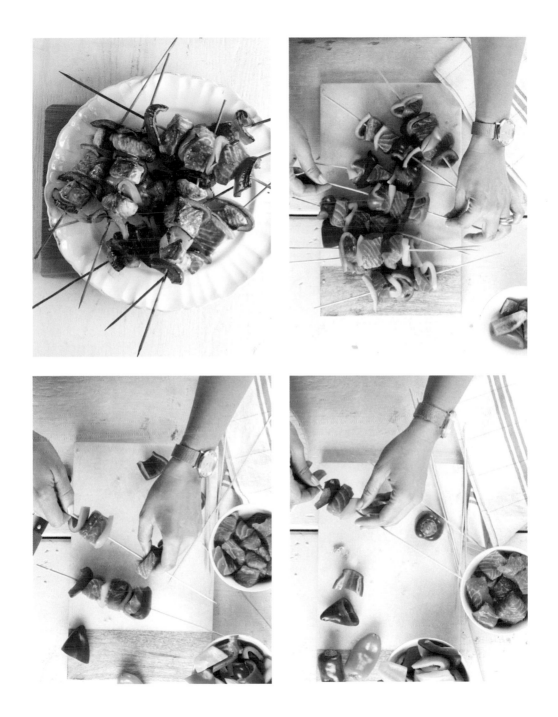

15 MINS

BLW **V**

SESAME CHICKPEA WRAPS WITH LIME & CORIANDER HUMMUS

| MAKES 6-8 WRAPS |

So much more flavour than a regular wrap, these Indian inspired 'socca' wraps are easy to make and have the goodness of the chickpeas running through them. Plus, kids seem to adore this healthy dip, and it's a fabulous quick-to-make party or picnic number. It's protein and fibre rich, and has high levels of iron and potassium, and magnesium for bone strength.

FOR THE BATTER

1 cup (100g) gram (chickpea) flour
1 cup (250ml) water
1 tbsp sesame seeds
1 tsp sesame oil or olive oil, plus extra for frying
pinch sea salt

FOR THE FILLING

2 cups chickpeas, soaked overnight and cooked, or 2 ×400g tins chickpeas, rinsed and drained
3 tbsp tahini paste
1 tsp ground coriander
2 garlic cloves
1 tbsp Dijon mustard
zest and juice of 1 lime
60ml olive oil
large coriander sprig, roughly chopped
salt and pepper
sliced crudité to serve

Whisk the ingredients for the pancakes together and let the batter sit for a few minutes while you get the filling ready.

Place the chickpeas, tahini, ground coriander, garlic, mustard, lime zest and juice in the bowl of a food processor, and pulse-blend until smooth. Drizzle the oil in while the blades are running, then gradually pour in the water until you have a smooth, paste-like consistency. Add salt and pepper and coriander and blitz until green!

Heat a little oil in a frying pan and add a ladleful of the batter, tilting it in the pan to form an even, thin layer. Fry for 2 minutes on each side, then remove to a plate and smooth the hummus over the top. Repeat with the remaining batter and then scatter with your chosen crunchy vegetables (I love carrot, avocado, red pepper and cucumber) before wrapping and eating.

Fresh coriander is a digestive aid; it balances blood sugar and has natural antibacterial and immunity-enhancing oils

VEG BLW D

SWEETCORN & BABY LEEK FRITTERS

| MAKES 12 FRITTERS |

These are a crunchy, fluffy delight of a bite. A super-fast batch of fritters that works as everyone's supper, as well as for lunchboxes in the week – the perfect time-saving treat. Crunchy with pops of fresh corn and flecks of sweet leeks, kids seem to go wild for them. Fresh sweetcorn is full of betacarotene and lutein for lovely hair and skin, and does great things for your digestive tract. The uncooked leeks are really great for giving your stomach bacteria a massive boost of prebiotics, with antibacterial and anti-inflammatory goodness too.

1 corncob
½ cup (60g) gluten-free bread
    flour
½ tsp baking powder
2 tbsp grated Parmesan cheese
2 eggs
60ml milk
2 baby leeks, finely sliced
2 tbsp olive oil
salt and pepper

Bring a pan of water to the boil, add the corncob and cook for 10 minutes, or until tender. Remove from the heat and leave to cool briefly.

Put the flour, baking powder and Parmesan in a bowl and whisk together.

Shave the corn kernels from the cob and reserve half of them. Put the other half in a food processor with the eggs and milk, and whizz until almost smooth. Fold this wet mixture into the dry ingredients, along with the reserved whole corn kernels and leeks, until combined. Season with salt and pepper to taste.

Heat the oil in a frying pan and spoon smallish puddles of the batter into it, frying for a couple of minutes until browned then flipping and repeating until done. Although these fritters are best eaten warm, they can be frozen once cooked and then warmed up individually, in the oven or pan, as and when needed.

BLACK BEAN & PAPRIKA CHICKEN QUESADILLAS

| SERVES 4 |

My kids had never tried this recipe before I wrote it for this book, but it went down really well, so I hope it works for yours too. Black beans are abundant in iron, which is crucial for carrying oxygen to red blood cells, and molybdenum which is key for a healthy liver and releasing iron in the body.

FOR THE BLACK BEANS
2 tbsp rapeseed oil
2 red onions, sliced
2 garlic cloves, minced
1 tbsp ground coriander
3 tbsp chopped coriander
400g tin black beans
2 red peppers, deseeded and
    sliced
100g sun-dried tomatoes

FOR THE PAPRIKA CHICKEN
2 tbsp rapeseed oil
1 onion, finely sliced
2 garlic cloves, finely chopped
1 tsp sweet smoked paprika
2 × 400g tins plum tomatoes
½ cup (125ml) chicken or
    vegetable stock (page 74)
2 cups (300g) cooked chicken
    meat

TO SERVE
olive oil, for frying
10–14 gluten-free corn tortillas
1 cup (125g) grated Cheddar

To make the beans, heat the oil in a large, deep pan and add the onions, garlic, ground coriander and coriander stalks, stirring occasionally for about 5 minutes until the onions are translucent but not browned. Be careful with the garlic as it can catch easily. Drain the beans, reserving 200ml of the liquid and add both to the pan with the red peppers. Stir through and cook over medium-low heat for 5 minutes. Roughly chop the sun-dried tomatoes, add to the pan and cook for a few extra minutes to give them a chance to break down.

For the chicken, heat the oil in a saucepan and add the onion, garlic and paprika. Cook over medium-low heat for 5–10 minutes to fully soften the onions. Stir in the tomatoes, pour in the stock and bring to the boil. Reduce the heat and let it bubble away gently for 15 minutes, stirring occasionally. Add the chicken and allow to warm through for a few minutes.

Heat a teaspoon of olive oil in a small frying pan, add a single tortilla and heat for 2 minutes on each side. Repeat with the remaining tortillas and pile them up. Transfer a tortilla to a plate and cover with the filling, either beans or chicken, and cheese if using, and place another tortilla on top. Turn over and press down to create a compact sandwich. Serve sliced into halves or quarters.

35 MINS

BLW N

CHICKEN CASHEW SATAY SKEWERS WITH GREEN RICE

| SERVES 4 |

The idea behind these satay skewers was to get across the gorgeous curry flavours, especially for my husband, without a bubbling pot. The cashews make the sauce unbelievably creamy and they add a sweetness, too. A make-ahead number for fast suppers or picnics that also freezes really well.

2 tbsp coconut oil
1 onion, diced
2 carrots, diced
½ tsp ground cinnamon
½ tsp sweet smoked paprika
1 tsp garam masala
1 cup (135g) cashews
1 cup (250ml) chicken stock
   (page 74)
3 chicken breasts, approx.
   400g, chopped into 2.5cm
   chunks
1 tbsp sesame oil
1 tbsp sesame seeds

FOR THE GREEN RICE
300g brown basmati rice
2 tbsp olive oil
2 tbsp chopped coriander
3 spring onions, finely sliced
salt

KIT:
8–10 bamboo skewers, soaked
in water

Preheat the oven to 180°C/350°F/Gas mark 4. Heat 1 tablespoon of oil in a heavy-based pan or casserole dish. Add the onion, carrots and spices and gently sauté over medium heat for about 7 minutes until the vegetables start to soften. Tip in the cashews and the chicken stock and bring to the boil. Reduce the heat to medium-low and simmer for 10 minutes. Tip into a blender or food processor and whizz for 1–2 minutes until really smooth. Add a little more stock or water if needed, to aid blending. You're looking for a dollop texture: not runny, but not a paste.

Cook the rice as per instructions, for roughly 20 minutes.

In a clean pan, heat the remaining 1 tablespoon oil on medium-high heat and sear the chicken pieces until browned on all sides. Thread the chicken pieces onto the skewers, drizzle with the sesame oil, spoon some of the sauce over and sprinkle with sesame seeds. Place on a baking sheet lined with baking paper and cook in the oven for 15 minutes until the chicken is cooked through. Drizzle the olive oil over the cooked rice and season with salt. Sprinkle over the coriander and spring onions and mix well. Remove the skewers from the oven. Plate the green rice and skewers and spoon over more of the cashew sauce, reheating it if needed.

THAI 'POW' CHICKEN BITES WITH SWEET CHILLI DIPPING SAUCE & SWEET POTATO FLATBREADS

| MAKES 20 LITTLE PATTIES & 8 FLATBREADS |

Recently visiting my great friend, we were given a plateful of the kids' leftovers, made by a Thai kitchen whizz, Pao, and we all inhaled them. This is my attempt.

FOR THE DIPPING SAUCE
2 garlic cloves
1 small red chilli
½ red pepper, deseeded and
    roughly chopped
¼ cup (60ml) rice vinegar
¼ cup (60ml) maple syrup
2 tsp tapioca flour (or arrowroot)
    mixed with 1 tbsp water

FOR THE FLATBREADS
1 medium-sized sweet potato
½ cup (50g) gram (chickpea)
    flour, plus extra for dusting
¾ cup (120g) buckwheat flour
juice of ½ lemon
1 leek, very finely sliced
½ tsp fennel seeds
½ tsp ground turmeric

Preheat the oven to 200°C/400°F/Gas mark 6. Put the sweet potato on a baking tray and roast in the oven for 50 minutes, until very soft.

Make the dipping sauce – this can be made days ahead. Put the garlic, chilli, red pepper, vinegar and 125ml water in a food processor or blender and whizz until completely broken down. Scrape the contents into a small saucepan and bring to a gentle simmer. Add the maple syrup and simmer for 5–7 minutes until fragrant and starting to thicken. Add the tapioca and water mixture, stir well and let it bubble very gently for another 1–2 minutes, watching carefully as it will thicken up fairly fast. Remove from the heat and leave to cool. Store in a bottle or jar in the fridge (keeps for 3 weeks).

To make the flatbreads, scoop out the flesh from the sweet potato and mash it in a large bowl with a fork until totally smooth. Add the remaining ingredients and combine gently until no floury patches remain. Make a ball of the dough and wrap tightly in cling film. Leave to firm up in the fridge for at least 30 minutes.

Meanwhile, make the chicken bites. Throw the ingredients in a large bowl and use your hands (wear gloves if you prefer) to

1 tbsp almond oil

large pinch sea salt

FOR THE CHICKEN BITES

500g minced chicken (mixed white and dark meat)

2 shallots, very finely sliced

1 tbsp sweet basil leaves, finely chopped

1 tsp fish sauce

1 tbsp kaffir lime leaves, very finely chopped

1 cup (125g) green beans, sliced into 1cm rounds

1 tbsp red curry paste (or tomato purée)

work everything in well. Form into golf balls and then press down to flatten. Put on a tray and chill in the fridge.

Remove the sweet potato bread dough from the fridge and divide the dough into four balls. Roll each ball into a circle about 18cm wide, using flour to prevent sticking.

Take the chicken bites out of the fridge and heat a little oil in a frying pan over medium-high heat. Add the patties and fry for 4–5 minutes on each side until golden and cooked through. Remove and keep warm.

Heat a little oil in a clean, small frying pan over medium heat and fry each flatbread, in turn, for about 45 seconds per side until browned. Add more oil as needed so the pan doesn't dry out. Serve the flatbreads topped with the chicken bites along with some green leaves and the dipping sauce alongside.

Give the chicken mince a good massage – the longer you do, the better the flavour, and the easier they will stick together in balls

V

JAMMY CRANBERRY OAT SLICES

| MAKES 1 TRAY |

A one-bowl, one-tray bake, these fruity bites are heaven with a cup of tea, and perfect for a grab-and-go tummy filler. They are juicy and filling, with a lovely cranberry tang. Oats are a fabulous blood-sugar-stabilising energy source, keeping tummies full without the sugar crash. There are always more snacks needed in our house! And when they're this easy to make, and so delicious, you can't help making them again.

½ cup (75g) dried dates, chopped

1 cup (150g) dried cranberries, roughly chopped

3 cups (270g) oats

¼ cup (30g) buckwheat groats

¼ cup (30g) quinoa flakes

1 tbsp linseeds

1 tsp ground cinnamon

pinch sea salt

½ cup (50g) raw honey

⅔ cup (75g) coconut oil or butter

Preheat the oven to 180°C/350°F/Gas mark 4. Line a 12 inch square baking tray with baking paper.

Place the dates and cranberries in a small bowl and pour over enough boiling water to cover. Leave to steep for a few minutes. Drain the fruit, reserving the liquid, and heat gently in a saucepan with 2–4 tablespoons water until very soft, about 5 minutes. Set aside.

In a bowl, mix together the oats, buckwheat groats, quinoa flakes, linseeds, cinnamon and salt. Melt the honey and oil or butter in a small saucepan over low heat, then pour onto the oat mixture and combine with a wooden spoon until everything is coated.

Tip half the mixture into the prepared baking tray, pressing down firmly with a spatula to form an even layer. Spread the cranberry mixture on top, and finish with the final layer of oats, being sure to press firmly again. Bake for 10–15 minutes, until golden brown and crisping at the edges. Leave to cool and slice into pieces. They keep for up to a week in a sealed container.

30 MINS

BLW **V**

CHIA OATCAKES

| MAKES 20 OATCAKES |

A great, tasty, savoury crunch, these gems work after school, after supper or in between, and they are so easy. With hummus, cheese or avocado, they're a vehicle for so much goodness too. Oats are full of nutrients and have more fibre than other grains, thus slowing absorption and preventing blood sugar spikes, with magnesium also regulating insulin secretion. They're easily digested and great for easing upset tummies, with all the super powers of chia seeds: omega fatty acids, protein, iron and calcium. Nutrition bomb biscuits for anytime.

2 tbsp chia seeds
2 cups (180g) rolled oats
1 cup (90g) porridge oats
½ tsp sea salt
½ tsp cayenne pepper
  (optional)
½ cup (75g) butter or
  coconut oil

Preheat the oven to 200°C/400°F/Gas mark 6. Place the chia seeds in a small bowl with 60ml water and leave to swell.

Whizz the rolled oats in a food processor until crumbly in texture, add to the porridge oats, salt and cayenne, if using, and combine. Scatter on a large baking tray and toast in the oven for 5 minutes or so while you get on with the rest of the recipe.

Add the butter or oil to the chia seeds and pour over 60ml boiling water. Whisk together quickly to melt the butter or oil. Remove the oats from the oven and combine with the buttery liquid until a dough ball is formed. Place on a sheet of cling film or baking paper, with another layer on the top, and roll out to about 4mm thick. Cut out round cookie shapes and then carefully transfer them to a baking sheet lined with baking paper.

Bake for 10–12 minutes, rotate the tray to get an even bake on your cakes and continue to bake for another 10 minutes, or until nicely golden brown. Eat with hummus (recipe overleaf). Keeps for up to a week in an airtight container.

35 MINS

BLW **V**

ROASTED CARROT HUMMUS

| MAKES APPROX 2 X 200G JARS |

Children adore dipping and dunking and choosing their foods, and hummus is a great one to have in the fridge for any occasion. This beautifully sweet version, with an amazing caramelised carrot flavour, is a winner with kids for picnic time and for grown-ups at aperitif hour. And it's groaning with goodness: turmeric is a super-powerful antioxidant, with its potent ingredient curcumin shown to prevent the growth of some cancer cells. Iron and magnesium rich, this should prevent hunger pangs at the school gates as well as fuelling afternoons on rugs in the sunshine.

400g carrots, sliced into
    2-inch rounds
2 tbsp olive oil, plus ¼ cup
2 cups (400g) chickpeas,
    soaked overnight and cooked
    or 2 x 400g tins drained
    chickpeas
3 tbsp tahini paste
1 tsp turmeric
2 garlic cloves
1 tbsp Dijon mustard
juice of 1 lemon
3 tbsp water
sea salt and pepper

Preheat the oven to 180°C/350°F/Gas mark 4. Place the chopped carrots on a large baking tray, drizzle with 2 table-spoons of olive oil and sprinkle over some sea salt. Roast for 30 minutes, until they are starting to brown and caramelise. Leave to cool a little.

Place the slightly cooled carrots, chickpeas, tahini, turmeric, garlic cloves, mustard and lemon juice in the small bowl of a food processor and pulse until smooth. Drizzle in the remaining oil while the blades are still running. Add the water until it forms a smooth, paste-like consistency. Add salt and pepper to taste.

CHIA FLAX CRACKERS WITH ROASTED BEETROOT & GARLIC DIP

| MAKES APPROX 28 CRACKERS |

A super-fast, superfood-filled snack that is a hit with kids and adults alike. And they're nut free. When you need that satisfying crunch to dip with, or to cover with avocado, cheese or anything else, these are the best all-purpose beauties. They have a lovely nutty flavour, and bags of goodness – chia and linseeds are the base here, and they provide a massive omega 3 hit, as well as a gut-loving digestion aid and lots of protein and iron.

FOR THE CRACKERS

1 cup (150g) linseeds

2 tbsp chia seeds

2 tbsp sunflower seeds

3 tbsp pumpkin seeds

2 tbsp pine nuts

1 tsp sea salt

1 tbsp za'atar (or mixed dried rosemary, thyme and salt)

1 tbsp cayenne (adds a lovely heat, but not for the littlies)

Place all the ingredients in a bowl with 250ml water and leave for 15 minutes. The seeds will absorb the water and become jelly-like.

Preheat the oven to 180°C/350°F/Gas mark 4. Line two baking trays with baking paper and spread the seeds evenly between the trays. Use a spatula and spread as thinly as possible, without any holes forming (if holes form, just patch up with a little of the seed mixture). Score them in to squares very lightly on the surface with a sharp knife (this makes breaking them up easier later).

Bake for 15 minutes, then very carefully flip the whole layer over and bake for a further 10 minutes to ensure it is all really crispy. Snap pieces off and store in an airtight container for up to 5 days. They are crispest on the first day, so do pop them back in the oven to regain their crunch. ➤

BLW V

Beetroot & Garlic Dip

4 medium beetroots

5 garlic cloves

2 tbsp olive oil

1 tbsp tahini

juice of 1 lemon

½ tsp cumin powder

1 tsp Dijon mustard

splash apple cider vinegar

salt and pepper

2 springs of parsley

Preheat the oven to 170°C/340°F/Gas mark 3½. Roast the whole beetroots and garlic cloves in the oven drizzled with oil and a splash of water on a tightly foil-covered baking tray for about 45 minutes. Check with a fork that they're soft in the middle.

Leave to cool and then peel and roughly chop. Add them to the food processor with the remaining ingredients and blitz until smooth and thick. Add a couple of sprigs of parsley towards the end and season to taste. Trickle in a little water if the consistency is still too thick, depending on the water content of your beetroots. Keeps in jars in the fridge for a week at least.

Lizzie ♥ The eye-popping colour of beetroot is where the betacyanin antioxidant power comes from, rich in iron too, this combo helps increase oxygen uptake in the blood, for more vitality and energy

40 MINS

BLW **N** **V**

EASY QUINOA LOAF

| MAKES 1 LOAF |

Since giving up gluten, this tasty, fluffy loaf has been the Holy Grail. The gluten-free world is not a friend to bread. Most shop-bought versions are either massively dense, too crumbly or full of sugars and preservatives to make them taste halfway decent. But this quinoa loaf is both fluffy and soft in the middle, with enough of a crust at the edges too. Don't be scared off by the ingredients list, or thinking the rest will go to waste. They won't, because you'll be making this super-simple loaf again and again.

FOR THE DRY INGREDIENTS

1 cup (120g) quinoa flour
½ cup (60g) tapioca flour
½ cup (50g) gram (chickpea) flour
½ cup (50g) quinoa flakes
1 tsp baking powder
1 tsp bicarbonate of soda
½ tsp xantham gum
1 tsp sea salt
½ cup (70g) sunflower seeds

FOR THE WET INGREDIENTS

3 eggs
2 tsp apple cider vinegar
250ml almond milk
2 tbsp olive oil
1 tbsp maple syrup

Preheat the oven to 180°C/350°F/Gas mark 4. Line a 900g loaf tin with baking paper.

In a large bowl, combine the dry ingredients, reserving 2 tablespoons of sunflower seeds. In a separate bowl, lightly beat the eggs with a fork and then add the remaining wet ingredients and mix together.

Make a well in the dry ingredients and pour in the wet ingredients. Fold in thoroughly using a wooden spoon, but try not to overwork the dough. It should be quite a thick dough that is still pourable.

Tip the bread dough into your prepared loaf tin. Sprinkle over the reserved sunflower seeds evenly, or in a pretty pattern if you want to be fancy.

Bake in the oven for 35 minutes until well risen above the tin and a golden brown crust has formed on top. Leave to cool in the tin for at least 5 minutes before turning out onto a wire rack to cool completely. Slice up and eat warm; try it with my Roasted Hazelnut Chocolate Butter Spread (page 212). This keeps for 5 days and toasts up a dream.

ROASTED HAZELNUT CHOCOLATE BUTTER SPREAD

| MAKES A 250G JAR |

This is a totally delicious chocolatey treat that's a one-whizz cinch packed with goodies for skin, hair, red blood cells and energy. Shop-bought chocolate spreads are a junk-filled disaster with mainly sugar and palm oil to bulk them out. But try this gem and keep chocolate deliciousness on your toast and pancakes or best straight from the jar with a spoon. It's a finger-licking health kick! Give it a whizz and try not to eat it all in one go!

1½ cup (210g) skin-on hazelnuts

¾ cup (100g) macadamia nuts

4 level tbsp cacao powder (or cocoa)

60ml maple syrup

2 tbsp rice syrup (or use maple syrup)

1 tbsp coconut oil

1 tsp vanilla extract

pinch sea salt flakes

Preheat the oven to 170°C/340°F/Gas mark 3½. Lay the nuts on a baking tray and roast for 10–12 minutes until the skins start to darken. Leave to cool slightly. Tip the nuts onto a tea towel, rub until most of the skins fall off – they will just shed, it's not a fiddle, I promise.

Place the nuts in the bowl of a food processor and whizz for about 5 minutes, until they break down into a nut butter. Add the cacao powder and pulse-blend until combined. Add the maple and rice syrups, oil, vanilla extract and salt and pulse briefly. Drizzle in a little warm water to help the butter along; it should be spreadable in consistency. Keeps in a jar in the fridge for up to 2 weeks, if there's no one home!

POPCORN TWO WAYS

| MAKES ONE BIG SHARING BOWL |

Friday night in our house involves PJs, a movie and bowls of warm popcorn made to order! A far cry from the gargantuan buckets of sugar-dripping corn you get at the movies, this is so straightforward to make but also packs a nutritional punch. The plant superpowers called polyphenols, which neutralise free radicals and keep your cells healthy, are higher in popcorn than in almost all fruit! And the added flavour bombs, whether you're a fan of savoury or sweet, are an easy whisk-up with goodies in them too.

FOR THE POPCORN

Warm 1 tsp ghee or coconut oil in a large pan over medium heat. Add ½ cup (90g) corn kernels and toss until thoroughly coated in the oil. Cover with the lid and turn the heat down to low, shaking vigorously as the corn begins to pop to stop it from sticking. Remove from the heat when the popping sound slows to one every few seconds and then add your flavours below.

Caramel Crunch Popcorn

3 tbsp coconut oil (or butter)
1 tbsp almond butter
3 tbsp rice syrup
pinch sea salt
1 tsp vanilla extract

In a small saucepan, heat the coconut oil, almond butter, rice syrup and salt until just bubbling. Remove from the heat, stir in the vanilla carefully and toss through the popped corn. Serve warm.

Salt & Vinegar Popcorn

2 tbsp butter
1 tbsp rapeseed oil
1½ tbsp white balsamic vinegar
1 tsp sea salt flakes

In a small saucepan, melt the butter with the rapeseed oil, then whisk in the vinegar and salt. Drizzle over the popcorn and toss together well. Serve warm.

ENERGY BITES

My kids have gone a little crazy for energy balls, and as my eldest normally 'hates nuts', I'm capitalising on this by trying out new ones.

The instant gratification of whizzing them up and munching on them is never lost on me, or my children, and we now have a vast number of different taste combinations to choose from. They are energy-packed and easy for little mouths to nibble on, as well as being utterly delicious. And the perfect ball to pack up for eating out, wherever you are. They live in the freezer, so you can have a stash on hand all the time!

BUILD-A-BITE Pick n' Mix

This is a foolproof 'map' to creating delicious nuggets in minutes. Your kids can join in and play around with the flavours to make a different 'bite' every time. Simply choose a texture, pair it with a hint of sweetness, a flavour sensation, something to bind it together and finally coat.

BUILD-A-BITE
CHART

texture

| Almonds | Cashews | Walnuts |
| Pecans | Hazelnuts | Oats |

fruit

| Dates | Prunes | Cranberries |
| Dried apricots | Raisins | Dried figs |

binder

| Almond butter | Rice syrup | Tahini |
| Coconut oil | Cashew butter | Maple syrup |

flavour

| Cacao | Lime zest | Cinnamon |
| Vanilla | Coconut | Ginger |

rolled in

Shredded coconut   Melted chocolate
Ground almonds   Cinnamon
Chia seeds

Caramel Cashew Balls

1 cup (135g) cashews
1 cup (140g) almonds
pinch sea salt flakes
½ cup (90g) dried apricots, roughly chopped
2 dates, pitted and roughly chopped
3 tbsp almond butter
1 tsp vanilla extract

Put the nuts in the bowl of a food processor with the salt and whizz until you have a fine meal. Add the apricots and dates and pulse-blend until combined. Add the almond butter and vanilla, and pulse again to form a ball. Add a trickle of water to help it come together if needed. Roll into balls and freeze in an airtight bag.

Lime & Coconut Balls

¼ cup (40g) pistachios
½ cup (70g) cashews
1 cup (140g) almonds
zest and juice of 1 lime
zest of ½ lemon
½ cup (25g) desiccated coconut, plus extra for dusting
2 dates
2 tbsp coconut oil
2 tbsp rice syrup

Blend the nuts in a food processor until they are a rough meal. Add in the zest, desiccated coconut and pulse until combined. Finally add in the dates, coconut oil, syrup and lime juice until a sticky ball forms. Peel off tablespoonfuls and roll into balls. Dust the balls in the extra coconut and place in the freezer to harden. Store there for up to 4 months.

5 MINS

N BLW **V**

Carrot Cake Bombs

1 cup (120g) walnuts
1 cup (110g) pecans
1½ tsp ground cinnamon
½ tsp ground ginger
pinch sea salt flakes
4 dates, pitted and roughly chopped
1 carrot, finely grated
2 tbsp almond butter
1 tsp vanilla extract
1 tbsp maple syrup

Put the nuts, spices and salt in the bowl of a food processor and whizz until you have a fine meal. Add the dates and pulse-blend until combined. Add the carrot, almond butter, vanilla extract and maple syrup and pulse again to form a ball. Add a trickle of water to help it come together if needed. Roll into balls; can be frozen for up to 2 months.

Red Velvet Bombs

1 cup (110g) pecans
1 cup (140g) almonds
2 tbsp beetroot powder, plus extra for dusting
2 tbsp cacao powder
4 dates, pitted and roughly chopped
pinch of salt
1 tsp vanilla extract
1 tsp rice syrup – add more to taste for sweetness,
    if needed
1 tbsp almond butter

Pulse the nuts in a food processor to form a crumbly texture – about a minute or two. Add the beetroot and cacao powder and roughly chopped dates and pulse until combined. Add a pinch of salt and the vanilla extract, rice syrup and almond butter and pulse until a ball forms. Pull off tablespoon-size pieces and roll into balls, dust with more beautiful beetroot powder and freeze until firm. Alternatively, flatten into a tin and freeze, chopping up into brownie squares later. Store in the freezer for up to 2 months.

PUDDINGS & CAKES

I'm no natural baker. I find the precision and alchemy required isn't really my style, but as always, greed steers me, and I love a good treat to round off a meal. So I've devised my own way of making cakes and treats that doesn't rely on such watertight weights and measures.

Here is my ever-growing hit list of goodies, all of which are easy to put together and are pretty resilient in terms of the accuracy of your timings and measurements. There is no need to be a perfectionist, unless you can't help it! These recipes will work even if you don't meticulously weigh every single item; they are designed to taste amazing with minimal hassle.

With fresh fruit as the cornerstone of so much that is good for you and crucial for growing children, it's simple to weave into puddings to give them a boost and make them taste fabulous. Molten apple and bursting berries are such different creatures to their uncooked versions. All types are used here to add flavour, sweetness and nature's bounty of goodness as simply as possible. These puddings are decadent enough for a celebration, delicious enough for a dinner party, and so full of health you can have the leftovers for breakfast.

FRESH ORANGE JUICE JELLY BOATS

| MAKES 21 BOATS |

Our lovely Nanny first made these for us, and now they're number one at every party I do for my kids – always asked for, and always hoovered up by every child. Most of them try to take a few home, their soggy orange pockets the ultimate giveaway. They look so pretty sailing across the table as little orange boats, and taste so fabulously fresh I guarantee they're worth the orange squeezing!

8 gelatine leaves
approx. 5 large navel oranges
(enough to make 500ml
freshly squeezed orange
juice)
2 tbsp coconut sugar

KIT:
21 cocktail sticks
wrapping paper to decorate

Soak the gelatine leaves in a bowl with 250ml cold water until they are very soft.

Halve the oranges and juice them to get 500ml orange juice. Place the juice in a small saucepan with the coconut sugar and bring to the boil. Remove from the heat.

Squeeze the water out of the gelatine leaves and add them to the warm orange mixture, stirring to dissolve completely.

Hollow out the orange halves you have juiced, removing any remaining pith but being careful not to make holes in them (these will be your 'boats'). Place them in a small tray or Tupperware container that will fit in your fridge, and pour the juice in almost to the top of each orange half. Chill in the fridge for at least 2 hours to set. If made ahead, they keep really well in the fridge for a few days.

Lizzie ♥ Gelatin is a skin, nail and hair booster, and also contains glycine which calms and helps kids sleep

When you are ready to serve them, cut each half into quarters, and place a cocktail stick into the centre of the jelly, with a triangle of wrapping paper skewered through it, so it looks like a sailing boat.

VEG BLW N

RASPBERRY BAKED OATMEAL

| MAKES 12 SQUARES |

The best hybrid of breakfast, pudding and a packed snack there is, these chewy treats are also the perfect thing for kids to help out with and stir, as nothing can go too badly wrong!

1 cup (90g) rolled oats
¼ cup (25g) quinoa flakes
2 tbsp milled flaxseeds
¼ cup (40g) walnuts
2 tbsp buckwheat groats
¼ cup (40g) coconut sugar
1 tsp ground cinnamon
2 eggs, beaten
250ml oat milk
½ cup (80g) frozen raspberries (or any berries you have to hand), plus extra

Preheat the oven to 170°C/340°F/Gas mark 4. Line a 25cm rectangular baking tray with baking paper.

Combine the dry ingredients, except the groats, in a bowl, tip in the eggs and milk and stir together. Tumble in the berries and combine – you should get lovely pink streaks as the raspberries bleed into the mixture. Scrape into the prepared tray, spreading the mixture evenly and right into the corners. Sprinkle with the buckwheat groats and stud with a few more berries to decorate. Bake for 40 minutes until browning and firm to the touch.

Allow to cool in the tin slightly and then slice into bars or squares. Keeps well for up to a week in an airtight container.

Lizzie ♡ Cinnamon is warm and naturally sweet with amazing anti-microbial properties and has been shown to balance blood sugar levels

20 MINS

V

BUTTER TOFFEE APPLES

| MAKES 6-8 TOFFEE APPLES |

Sticky, crunchy and so juicy underneath, these taste a little like a buttered apple pie on a stick. A 10-minute job that you will get a ton of love for – my kids squealed when they first clapped eyes on them.

Apples are a fabulous autumn munch, with tons of vitamin C and pectin and fibre that helps stabilise blood sugar. It's not sugar, but it is a sweet treat of stickiness so don't make them every day! There are goodies in these sweeteners too, which makes them a better addition than the empty white stuff. They're a fabulous bonfire-night trick to pull out.

6–8 small apples
125ml rice syrup
2 tbsp coconut oil or butter
½ cup (70g) coconut palm
    sugar
2 tbsp milk of choice (oat, rice,
    almond)
pinch sea salt
1 tsp vanilla extract
sesame seeds or chopped nuts
    (optional), to coat

KIT:
6–8 wooden lollipop sticks

Place the apples on a baking sheet lined with baking paper and pierce the lollipop sticks through the stalk end, about 2.5cm, so they are secure. Place in the fridge to chill.

In a small saucepan, gently heat the rice syrup, coconut oil or butter, coconut sugar and milk until combined. Turn the heat up a little and whisk everything as it starts to bubble. Leave it gently bubbling for 10 minutes, occasionally stirring. The mixture will thicken up gradually: when it coats the back of a wooden spoon thickly it's ready.

Remove from the heat, whisk in the salt and vanilla extract and work quickly to dunk the apples into the pan, swirling them through the toffee until coated. Dunk in the sesame seeds or chopped nuts, if using. Keep twirling the apples upright as the coating hardens, and then place on the baking sheet. Chill in fridge to harden.

STRAWBERRY CUSTARD TARTS

| MAKES 4 MINI-TARTS OR 1 × 20CM TART |

I've had a thing for French custard tarts since I was tiny. We lived opposite a Richoux patisserie, and they always had a mouth-watering display of pastries that we gazed longingly at.

So I wanted to make something with that crème pâtissière flavour, and the juicy, fresh strawberry, but with goodies in. These are so simple you'll never want to faff around with pastry and custard again!

200g fresh strawberries, hulled and sliced

FOR THE CASHEW CRÈME
1 cup (135g) cashews
1 tbsp lemon juice
2 tbsp maple syrup
1 tsp vanilla extract

FOR THE ALMOND CRUST
140g almonds
20g butter, melted
2 tbsp maple syrup
pinch sea salt

Soak the cashews in a bowl of water for at least 1 hour.

Preheat the oven to 180°C/350°F/Gas mark 4.

Make the crust. Blitz the almonds in a food processor until you have fine crumbs. Pour in the melted butter, maple syrup and salt and blitz until mixed. Tip the mixture into four loose-bottomed, mini-fluted tart tins or one 20cm tart tin and use fingertips to press and mould the pastry up the sides and into the bases of the tins. Bake for 10 minutes, until lightly golden. Remove and leave to cool slightly.

For the cashew crème, drain the cashews and put them in a food processor with the remaining ingredients. Whizz until you have a smooth and creamy mixture, and spoon over the almond crust. Use a knife to level out the surface, then lay sliced strawberries over the top in a pretty pattern.

VEG N D

CHESTNUT CHOCOLATE BROWNIES WITH CARAMEL SWIRLS

| MAKES 12-16 BROWNIES |

Everyone loves a brownie. But I know how many good recipes there are out there already, and I wasn't desperate to add another to the mountain! But then I was fiddling with flavours and flours one day, thinking how the Italians always get chestnut to work so well, and these happened. Dense and gooey with a caramel crunch and crust, they really are fabulous, and such a cinch to make. The caramel swirls take them up to the next level.

200g dark chocolate (70% cocoa solids minimum), chopped
170g butter
1 cup (100g) chestnut flour
½ cup (60g) gluten-free plain flour
½ tsp baking powder
1 tsp bicarbonate of soda
pinch sea salt
60ml honey
60ml maple syrup
1 tsp vanilla extract
3 eggs, beaten
¼ cup (50g) dark chocolate chips

FOR THE CARAMEL BUTTER SWIRL (OPTIONAL)
¼ cup (60g) almond butter
1–2 tbsp honey
2 tsp coconut oil
1 tsp vanilla extract

Preheat the oven to 180°C/350°F/Gas mark 4. Line a 25cm x 35cm rectangular baking tin with baking paper. Place the chopped dark chocolate and butter in a heatproof bowl suspended over a pan of simmering water (making sure the bowl isn't touching the water) and let them melt together slowly. Stir occasionally.

In a large bowl, combine both flours, the baking powder, bicarbonate of soda and salt. Remove the melted chocolate and butter from the heat. Stir in the honey, maple syrup and vanilla extract. Add the beaten eggs and stir quickly. Pour the wet ingredients into the dry and fold together just enough to mix thoroughly, but don't overwork the mix. Finally, fold in the chocolate chips.

For the caramel swirl, melt the ingredients in a small pan over low heat, whisking as you go until smooth. Add a splash or two of hot water to help the mixture soften to get a pourable consistency. Spoon blobs on top of the brownie mixture, using a knife to create swirls on the surface. Scrape the mixture into the prepared tin and bake for 15–18 minutes (maximum) until a skin develops on top but it is still wobbly in the centre. This is to keep that amazing gooeyness when it's cooled. Remove and leave to cool in the tin before cutting into squares.

QUINOA & RICE CHOC CRISPIES

| MAKES APPROX. 15 CRISPIES |

The glistening chocolate crispy cakes of so many people's childhoods, but with some tasty goodness and just as easy to get together. They are a regular at every party, and they work really well as Easter nests with eggs placed in the middle, and as Christmas party wreaths. Any celebration will be made better with some of these gooey, crunchy bites.

½ cup (100g) coconut oil
5 tbsp brown rice syrup
2 tbsp almond butter
¼ cup (25g) cacao powder
1 cup (20g) puffed quinoa
1 cup (20g) puffed brown rice

Melt the coconut oil in a small saucepan with the rice syrup, almond butter and cacao powder until just melted

Mix together the puffed quinoa and puffed brown rice, then pour over the warm mixture. Stir together until well mixed and sprinkle in a few extra of either of the puffed grains to clean the pan – you won't want to waste this elixir.

Scoop tablespoonfuls into mini-muffin cases and place them on a tray in the freezer for 10 minutes (or fridge for 1–2 hours).

They're best eaten on the day they are made, as they are much crunchier and more unctuous when fresh from the fridge. But they will keep for a day or two in an airtight container (not gonna happen!).

Lizzie ♥

Puffed quinoa adds extra protein. You can make your own by heating the grains, but they won't be as inflated or as crunchy

HAZELNUT CHOC CRUNCH WITH RASPBERRIES

| MAKES 8-10 SLICES |

Total chocolate heaven, they're a little like those Italian chocolates, 'Baci' (kisses), that were designed as a Valentine's Day pressie. They're a hazelnut bomb of deliciousness, and a perfect treat for everyone. These are full of roasted hazelnuts that are rich in folate, vitamins E and K, as well as the B vitamin biotin for lovely hair and skin, copper for red blood cell building and cacao for a load of beautiful antioxidants. Couldn't be easier or faster to put together. And you can keep a stash in the freezer to munch on when the mood takes you.

1 cup (135g) hazelnuts
½ cup (60g) pecans
2 heaped tbsp cacao powder
large pinch sea salt
5–6 Medjool dates, pitted and
    roughly chopped
1 tbsp almond butter
1 tsp maple butter (or 1 tbsp
    maple syrup)
handful of fresh or frozen
    raspberries, to decorate

FOR THE TOPPING
½ cup cacao butter
2 tbsp cacao powder
60ml maple syrup
pinch sea salt

OR:
150g dark chocolate (70% cocoa
solids minimum)

Preheat the oven to 180°C/350°F/Gas mark 4. Line a 900g loaf tin with baking paper.

Lay the hazelnuts on a baking sheet and roast for 5–10 minutes. Leave to cool, tip into a clean tea towel, then rub between your hands to shed the skins. Reserve a small handful of nuts and roughly chop them.

Place the remaining nuts in the bowl of a food processor along with the pecans, and pulse-blend until you have fine meal. Add the cacao powder, salt, dates, almond and maple butters, and pulse-blend again until everything is broken down and sticky. Tip the mixture into the loaf tin and press firmly and evenly. Place in the freezer while you make the chocolate topping.

To make the topping, melt the chocolate, if using. Alternatively, melt the ingredients in a small pan over low heat, stirring occasionally. Take the tin out of the freezer, pour the topping over the nut mixture, scatter over the reserved hazelnuts and adorn with raspberries. Return the tin to the freezer to store for at least 30 minutes and remove 10 minutes before eating. Or keep in the fridge, if eating immediately.

VANILLA & STRAWBERRY ICE CREAM WITH BUTTERSCOTCH SAUCE

| MAKES APPROX. 500ML |

The best possible reincarnation for the sad, brown bananas clogging up your fruit bowl, with the instant gratification of an ice cream, without fancy machines or hours of stirring. Bananas are high in potassium which balances electrolytes after exercise. And the list of ingredients here is eye-wateringly healthy compared to the store-bought versions. You won't be able to stop yourself making this on repeat.

6 very ripe bananas
1 tsp vanilla bean paste
60ml rice or almond milk
1 cup (180g) frozen or fresh
   strawberries

**FOR THE BUTTERSCOTCH
SAUCE**
3 tbsp coconut oil
60ml coconut nectar
2 tbsp rice syrup
1 tsp vanilla bean paste

TO SERVE
handful of fresh strawberries
fresh mint leaves

Peel and slice the bananas. Lay the slices out on a baking tray lined with baking paper, cover and freeze overnight.

Place the frozen banana, vanilla bean paste and a splash of the almond milk in a blender, and whizz using the tamper to keep it all moving, adding milk gradually until soft-serve texture is reached. Scoop out half of the ice cream as the vanilla portion, to serve with the butterscotch sauce.

Add the strawberries to the remaining mixture, whizz again and you have two-tone delicious and super-healthy ice cream in minutes.

For the butterscotch sauce, gently warm the ingredients in a small saucepan until combined. Fold through the ice cream and freeze if not eating immediately.

Serve with strawberries and mint leaves scattered over the top.

Lizzie ♡ For a fudgy caramel flavour, add 2 dates and 2 tablespoons almond butter

CHOCOLATE-COVERED VANILLA CREAM LOLLIES

| MAKES 8–10 LOLLIES |

Whatever the weather people love a creamy vanilla lolly with a crisp chocolate coating. These are super quick to get into the moulds and full of goodness and energy from cacoa, almonds and skin-glowing coconut. No E numbers, gums or fillers in sight.

FOR THE LOLLIES
250ml rice milk
2 tbsp coconut oil
1 tsp vanilla powder
2 tbsp almond butter
2 tbsp maple syrup

FOR THE COATING
½ cup (110g) cacao butter
¼ cup (25g) cacao powder
1 tsp vanilla extract
2 tbsp maple syrup
pinch sea salt
a handful of flaked nuts, seeds or
    coconut to decorate

KIT:
10 x wooden lollipop sticks
ice lolly moulds

Blend all of the ingredients for the lollies and pour into moulds. Leave to set, making sure to take out after 30 minutes to place the lolly sticks in.

Melt the cacao butter and then whisk in the cacao powder, vanilla, maple syrup and salt.

When the lollies are totally set firm, remove from the moulds and dip into the chocolate mixture to coat. Sprinkle with almonds, coconut or seeds as you fancy!

Place on a lined baking sheet in the fridge or freeze until needed.

BLW   N   V

JAMMY ALMOND HEART COOKIES

| MAKES APPROX. 14 COOKIES |

This was dreamed up as a treat to make with the kids for Valentine's Day. A deliciously crunchy biscuit with a jammy middle that takes no time to get into the oven. Forget the junk- and trans-fat-filled packet versions. These are super-simple, with nuts and fresh berries to pack a vitamin- and mineral-rich punch to your afternoon snack attack. And so pretty, you'll want to make them as presents.

½ cup (100g) butter or coconut oil

125ml maple syrup

1 cup (100g) ground almonds

1 cup (150g) rice flour

½ cup (40g) unsweetened shredded or desiccated coconut

pinch sea salt

¼ tsp almond extract

approx. ¼ cup (150g) raspberry or strawberry jam

KIT:
heart-shaped cutter

Preheat the oven to 180°C/350°F/Gas mark 4. Line a baking sheet with baking paper.

Melt the butter or oil in a small saucepan with the maple syrup. Take off the heat and leave to cool slightly.

In a bowl, combine the ground almonds, rice flour and shredded coconut and pour over the liquid mixture. Add the salt and almond extract. Mix thoroughly – it will seem quite wet and sticky, but have faith!

Lay a sheet of cling film or baking paper on the work surface. Place the dough in the middle and top with another layer of cling film or parchment. Roll the dough out to about 5mm thick. Cut out rounds with a cookie cutter and make small heart shapes in half of them. Transfer carefully to the prepared baking sheet and bake for 8–10 minutes, until lightly golden. Leave to cool on a wire rack where they will crisp up.

Dollop a teaspoon of the jam onto each of the whole cookies, spreading the jam around the centre evenly. Top with a heart-holed one, creating a sandwich of almond jamminess.

VEG **BLW** N

BUCKWHEAT BANANA CHOCOLATE CHIP BREAD

| MAKES 1 LOAF |

Super-simple and speedy to the oven, this loaf is pretty fast to finish off too. It's another great 'brown banana' solution – don't waste them, bake them! Buckwheat is a marvel of a flour, as it's packed with antioxidant flavonoids, loads of fibre and 8 essential amino acids, as well as good amounts of manganese and magnesium for bone-growth, plus slow-release carbohydrates to steady blood sugar levels. An easy cake with an immune boost is a winner for me.

½ cup (75g) buckwheat flour
½ cup (75g) rice flour
1 tsp bicarbonate of soda
½ cup (50g) ground almonds
large pinch sea salt
3 bananas
2 eggs
1 tsp vanilla extract
3 tbsp rice syrup
2 tbsp coconut sugar
¼ cup (40g) chocolate chips,
    plus extra to sprinkle
2 tbsp slivered almonds

Preheat the oven to 180°C/350°F/Gas mark 4. Line a 900g loaf tin with baking paper.

In a large bowl, combine the flours, bicarbonate of soda, ground almonds and pinch of sea salt.

In a separate bowl, mash the bananas until almost smooth, leave a little texture, then beat in the eggs and vanilla extract. Pour in the rice syrup and add the coconut sugar, then combine. Pour the wet ingredients into the bowl with the dry ingredients and gently fold together until just combined. Finally, add the chocolate chips and most of the almond slivers and fold through again.

Tip the mixture into the prepared loaf tin and sprinkle with the reserved slivered almonds and chocolate chips. Bake for 40–50 minutes, until golden brown and a skewer inserted into the centre comes out clean. Leave to cool in the tin before transferring to a wire rack to cool completely.

ORANGE ALMOND CUPCAKES WITH CHOCOLATE GANACHE

| MAKES 12 MINI CUPCAKES |

The beautiful, juicy, zesty oranges, almonds and chocolatey toppings of these cupcakes keep everyone happy. With antioxidants galore and all that immune-boosting vitamin C, almonds for the hair, and skin-loving levels of vitamin E, these are deliciously good for you.

2 cups (200g) ground almonds
4 tbsp buckwheat flour
2 tsp baking powder
zest of 2 oranges and juice of 1
¼ cup (40g) coconut sugar
4 eggs
¼ cup (60ml) maple syrup

FOR THE CHOCOLATE GANACHE

⅓ cup (50g) chopped dark chocolate
1 tbsp rice milk
1 tbsp cacao powder
400ml tin coconut milk, cold

KIT:

12-hole mini-muffin tray
mini-cupcake cases

Preheat the oven to 180°C/350°F/Gas mark 4. Line a 12-hole mini-muffin tray with mini-cupcake cases. In a large bowl, mix together the ground almonds, buckwheat flour, baking powder, orange zest and coconut sugar.

Crack the eggs into a small bowl, then, using a fork, beat together with the orange juice and maple syrup. Combine the wet ingredients with the dry ingredients until just coming together. Pour the mixture into the mini-cupcake cases and place in oven to bake for 15 minutes. Remove and leave to cool.

When the cupcakes are just about cooled, start making the ganache. Place the chocolate, milk and the cacao powder in a heatproof bowl suspended over a pan of simmering water (making sure the bowl isn't touching the water). Heat until fully melted, take off the heat and stir to combine.

Remove the coconut milk from the fridge and pour the watery liquid into a small jar to use for smoothies or sauces at a later date. Scrape the thick white solids into the chocolate mixture. The ganache will harden as it cools so try to ice the cupcakes as soon as they are cool enough and use orange zest pieces to decorate.

CHOCOLATE CHESTNUT CLOUD CAKE

| SERVES 10-12 |

The first person to try out this cake, a lovely American friend of mine said, 'Holy moly, I would make this for the Queen.' I figured it needed to be included in the book even if the Queen never got any. The Italian in me always wants to incorporate a little of their flavours into my kitchen, but their desserts can be quite alcohol-drenched and overly sweet for me – ice creams aside, of course. So here I thought about using that very Tuscan ingredient, chestnut, which sets off the flavour of the chocolate so well. This is a dense, fudgy, chocolate joy of a cake with the goodness of chestnuts too. It's pretty special.

200g dark chocolate (70% cocoa solids minimum)
50g butter
pinch sea salt
415g tin chestnut purée
4 eggs
100g honey
handful of fresh raspberries or seasonal berries, to decorate

FOR THE FROSTING
400ml tin coconut milk, cold
2 tbsp maple syrup
4 tbsp cacao powder

KIT:
23cm springform cake tin
electric whisk

Preheat the oven to 180°C/350°F/Gas 4. Line a 23cm springform cake tin with baking paper. Place the chocolate, butter and sea salt in a heatproof bowl suspended over a pan of simmering water (making sure the bowl isn't touching the water). Allow to melt gently, then remove from the heat.

Place the chestnut purée into your food processor and add the eggs and honey. Blitz to form a smooth purée. Tip this mixture into the melted chocolate and combine. Pour into the prepared cake tin and bake for 35–40 minutes, until the cake looks glossy and with only a slight crack on top.

Meanwhile, make the frosting. Remove the coconut milk from the fridge and pour the watery liquid into a small jar to use for smoothies or sauces at a later date. Scrape the thick white solids into a bowl along with the maple syrup and cacao powder. Use an electric whisk to beat the mixture until light and billowy. Leave in the fridge to firm up.

Once the cake has cooled completely, spread the frosting in an even layer over the top and stud with fresh raspberries, or seasonal berries.

VEG

VANILLA, BERRY & HONEY CREAM CELEBRATION CAKE

| SERVES 12 |

This is a fabulous celebration cake, a delicious, totally healthy revamp of a classic Victoria sponge that looks so beautiful and tastes as indulgent as it should. It was invented for my daughter, a girl who doesn't like sponge or cake but who is wild about berries and cream – and this was a breakthrough! Honey is a delicate addition to the sponge, and served with some vanilla cream and tons of fresh fruit, the cake is way sweet enough without bags of sugar.

250g butter or coconut oil
4 tbsp raw honey
4 eggs
1 tbsp vanilla
1 tsp apple cider vinegar
220g gluten-free flour blend
½ cup (60g) tapioca flour
1 tsp xanthan gum
1 tsp bicarbonate of soda
1½ tsp baking powder
1 tsp sea salt

FOR THE HONEY CREAM
285ml double cream, or 400ml
   tin coconut milk, cold
1 tsp vanilla bean paste
1 tbsp raw honey
150g berry jam
250g assorted raspberries or
   strawberries, chopped
250g redcurrants

KIT:
electric whisk

Preheat the oven to 180°C/350°F/Gas 4. Line a 20cm or 23cm cake tin with baking paper. Melt the butter or coconut oil with the honey in a small saucepan, and leave off the heat to cool slightly. Use an electric whisk to whip the eggs until they are light and pale, about 2 minutes, then slowly drizzle in the melted butter, vanilla and vinegar.

Sift the flours, xanthan gum, bicarbonate of soda, baking powder and pinch of sea salt into the wet mixture and slowly mix, being careful not to overmix as this will make the cake too dense. Pour into the prepared tin and bake for 20 minutes in the centre of the oven, until a skewer inserted into the cake comes out clean. Leave to cool on a wire rack in its tin for 5 minutes before carefully turning it out.

For the honey cream, use an electric whisk to beat the cream until fluffy in a large bowl. (If using coconut milk, remove from the fridge and drain the watery liquid. Scrape the thick white solids into a large bowl.) Add the vanilla and honey gradually and whip the mixture until firm enough to spread. Keep chilled in the fridge. Slice the cake carefully through the middle with a large bread knife and spread with a third of the cream on one side and berry jam on the other, then dot with the chopped berries. Replace the top half of the cake, spread thickly with the remaining cream, then decorate with redcurrants.

N V

RAW LEMON, LIME & RASPBERRY CHEESECAKE

| SERVES 8-10 |

A no-bake, no-junk cheesecake that takes ten minutes to assemble. It lives in the freezer too, so you can eat it during the week, or you can make lots of mini-cheesecakes that look really pretty for a party. You won't miss the cream or digestives from the bog-standard version, because this is lighter and tastier. It builds bones and adds collagen with a hit of calcium, magnesium, iron, zinc and folate. The citrus bonanza helps digestion, blood clotting and fights bacteria.

FOR THE BASE
1 cup (140g) almonds
½ cup (70g) sunflower seeds
½ cup (70g) mixture of milled
    flaxseeds and pumpkin seeds
pinch Himalayan sea salt
zest of ½ lemon
zest of ½ lime
1 cup (175g) pitted dates,
    roughly chopped
1 tbsp almond butter

FOR THE TOPPING
1½ cups (210g) cashews soaked
    in water for at least 1 hour or
    overnight
¼ cup (50g) coconut oil, melted
1 tsp vanilla paste
¼ cup (60ml) maple syrup
zest of 1 lime and juice of 2
zest of 1 lemon and juice of 2
2 cups (250g) fresh raspberries

Place the almonds, seeds, salt and lemon and lime zests in the food processor and blitz to a crumb-like texture. Add the dates and continue to blitz until they are broken down; add the almond butter and combine. Tip the mixture into a 23cm cake tin and use the back of a spoon to press it into an even layer, working the mixture a little up to the sides, too. Cover with cling film and freeze to keep cold while you make the topping.

Drain the cashews and put them in the food processor with the coconut oil, vanilla paste, maple syrup and citrus zests and juices. Blitz to form a smooth purée, adding a tablespoon or two of water if needed. Taste at this stage, and add more maple syrup if you like. Fold in half of the fresh raspberries. Pour the mixture into the tin on top of the base and spread to a smooth finish. Return to freezer for at least 1 hour to firm up.

Take the cheesecake out of the freezer about 10 minutes before serving, to allow it to come to room temperature. Decorate with the remaining fresh raspberries.

MEAL PLANS

Meal plans are a time-saving, organisational wonder for all parents. Over the page, you'll find your weekly meals worked out, whether you want to reboot after a period of excess, have a lazy week, or go meat-free. I've tried to make cooking on busy weeknights as easy as possible by suggesting that you use your weekends to prep some meals ahead – of course, it's optional, but it can be a real time-saver.

REBOOT WEEK

Whether you need a week of healthy eating post-Christmas or if the sugar load has got too high over Halloween or the summer holidays, here is a meal plan that will flatten mumma's tummy, banish the dark circles under the kids' eyes and get everyone back on the healthy eating track.

	Sunday	Monday	Tuesday
Breakfast	Roasted asparagus & prosciutto frittata (*page 51*)	Hazelnut choc shake (*page 60*)	Spiced apple quinoa porridge (*page 34*)
Lunch	Lemon roast chicken with orange & maple-roasted roots (*page 140*)	Sweet miso cod with wilted cabbage (*page 131*)	Miso chicken rice noodle soup (*page 80*)
Snack	(Sunday lunch pudding) Raspberry baked oatmeal (*page 228*)	Red velvet bombs* (*page 220*)	Apple slices with nut butter sandwiches
Supper	Hearty red lentil & sweet potato soup* (*page 81*)	Roast chicken & kale stir-fry (*page 142*)	Sausage, squash & lentil hotpot (*page 177*)

* = make a double batch to feed everyone on two occasions

Breakfasts and supper are for everyone, whereas lunch is mostly aimed at parent(s) at home while the kids are at school. Some suggestions can also be taken to the office!

Wednesday	Thursday	Friday	Saturday
Plum crumble shake (*page 64*)	Strawberry power pudding (*page 48*)	Mini granola fruit cups (*page 46*)	Banana blueberry buckwheat pancakes (*page 32*)
Sesame chickpea wraps with lime & coriander hummus* (*page 192*)	Hearty red lentil & sweet potato soup (*page 81*)	Cumin turkey & sweet potato pie* (*page 150*)	Spinach, sweet potato & red onion bhajis (*page 188*)
Red velvet bombs (*page 220*)	Carrot sticks with left-over lime & coriander hummus	Carrot cake bombs (*page 220*)	Jammy cranberry oat slices (*page 202*)
Fusilli Florentine (*page 96*)	Sweet potato, coconut & green bean curry (*page 115*)	Florentine fishcakes (*page 128*)	Cumin turkey & sweet potato pie (*page 150*)

LAZY WEEK

With life as hectic as it is, we all need as much help as we can get, but some weeks seem to be particularly chock full with no room for manouevre, so I came up with this plan to reduce stress levels, save as much time as possible, but also eat well.

	Sunday	Monday	Tuesday
Breakfast	Banana blueberry buckwheat pancakes (*page 32*)	Spinach & egg mini muffins* (*page 43*)	Passion fruit smoothi (*page 60*)
Lunch	Lemon roast chicken with orange & maple-roasted roots (*page 140*). Make 2 for cooking in the week	Hearty red lentil & sweet potato soup* (*page 81*)	Miso chicken rice noodle soup (*page 80*)
Snack	(Sunday lunch pudding) Raspberry baked oatmeal (*page 228*). *Make bone broth (page 74)*	Caramel cashew balls* (*page 219*)	Carrot cake bombs* (*page 220*)
Supper	Tangy prawn angel hair soup (*page 75*)	Roast chicken & kale stri-fry (*page 142*)	Five-vegetable beef ragu* (*page 94*)

= make a double batch to feed everyone on two occasions

By doubling up on a few ingredients you can get through a week of healthy eating without fussing over each individual meal for hours. For instance, roasting an extra chicken on Sunday with lunch, or making a larger quantity of a recipe in the slow-cooker means you have done all the hard work for a few evening meals in the week ahead. You can also make a stock from the chicken bones to provide the base for sauces and lovely lunchtime soups.

Wednesday	Thursday	Friday	Saturday
Spinach & egg mini muffins (*page 43*)	Coconut cherry burst (*page 66*)	Spiced apple quinoa porridge (*page 34*)	Spinach & egg mini muffins (*page 43*)
Hearty red lentil & sweet potato soup (*page 81*)	Sesame chickpea wraps with lime & coriander hummus* (*page 192*)	Hearty red lentil & sweet potato soup (*page 81*)	Proper fish & chips with tempura vegetables (*page 137*)
Raspberry baked oatmeal (*page 228*)	Caramel cashew balls (*page 219*)	Carrot cake bombs (*page 220*)	Chia oat cakes & hummus (*page 204*)
Braised beef & winter vegetables* (*page 162*)	Ragu plus red kidney beans over rice	Crispy polenta-crusted cod with summer slaw & tahini dressing (*page 126*)	Braised beef & winter vegetables (*page 162*)

APPENDIX: THE ESSENTIAL FOOD GROUPS

Compared to other mammals, human babies are not ready to spring into action when they are born. Their brains in particular are not fully formed, and they require the right balance of nutrients to ensure they grow, function and develop properly into independent beings.

Unlike young mammals who forage for themselves after they are weaned from their mother, human babies rely on us to be fed for a lot longer. As parents and carers we are wholly responsible for what babies and children put in their mouths, and that is an incredibly responsible position. Knowledge is power, so below you will find all the information on carbohydrates, fats, proteins, vitamins and minerals that children need at all stages of their growth and development.

FOOD GROUPS

There are two groups: macronutrients, which are proteins, fats and carbohydrates; and micronutrients, which are vitamins, minerals, enzymes, phytonutrients and water. The key to a healthy diet is to eat a variety of nutritious foods from each of the food groups, which will provide all the vitamins and minerals your body needs to function well, grow and flourish.

• PROTEIN

Proteins are the building blocks used to repair, build and maintain our cells. They are involved in the making of muscles, nerves, organs and hormones. They are made up of amino acids, nine of which are called 'essential', meaning we have to get them from food as we cannot make them ourselves (our bodies can synthesize the rest).

SOURCES: *Animal products such as meat, fish, milk, cheese and eggs are rich sources of protein. Grains such as quinoa and amaranth are also complete proteins. Most other wholegrains and pulses only contain some of the amino acids needed, so should be combined to provide the complete protein profile. Nuts and seeds also provide some protein.*

• FATS

In recent times, fat has been demonised, being considered dangerous and mainly responsible for obesity and heart disease. However, scientists and doctors have shown that there are many types of healthy fats that are crucial for us all to thrive. Some fats are no good to anyone, such as those often found in fast food, packaged cakes, crisps and biscuits, but unsaturated and even some quality saturated fats are a great addition to a healthy diet, particularly for babies and children.

High in energy and calories, babies and children need a higher proportion of fat than adults, as they are growing and expending energy faster. Their brains are developing at an astonishing rate – in the first year alone a baby's brain triples in size – and since brains are made up of 60 per cent fat, a high-fat diet (especially the essential fatty acid Omega-3) is necessary. Nature's first food, breast milk, is made of at least 50 per cent fat.

Paediatrician Dr Stephen Cowan believes that fat is the most important nutrient for children by far, particularly saturated animal fat and non-animal fat, such as coconut. Children need these fats for the development of the nervous system, their immune systems and later on for healthy development of hormone and reproductive systems.

Saturated and unsaturated fats are the primary sources of the critical fat-soluble vitamins A, D, E and K, and minerals such as calcium need vitamin D to aid absorption. Saturated fats fight infection and build immune health, whilst also providing padding and protection for organs. Saturated fats are also essential for digestion and hormonal development.

Omega-3 fatty acids found in oily fish, nuts, seeds and eggs are essential. Research has found a strong relationship between eating omega-3s and children's behaviour. These fatty acids positively influence the signals sent between the brain and the body, and can stabilise mood swings and improve concentration and behaviour.

SOURCES: *All animal meat, fish, eggs, milk, wholegrains, seeds, nuts, coconuts, pulses and sea vegetables. Avocado, nut and seed oils.*
AVOID: *Low-fat foods and skimmed milks for children – they need the fat and such products are often bulked up with sugars and unnecessary thickening and preserving agents and gums.*

- **CARBOHYDRATES**

This is fuel for our bodies. Broken down to its most basic form, glucose, it is what we need to burn to produce energy. Carbohydrates should, where possible, be whole and complex and not refined, which acts more like regular sugar in our system. Wholegrains have fats, protein and fibre as well as vitamins and minerals, whereas most of these are lost when they are refined. Refined white flour and sugar actually remove valuable nutrients from the body, such as magnesium, as they're digested.

SOURCES: *Fresh fruits and vegetables, wholegrains such as brown rice, oats, buckwheat, quinoa, beans and pulses.*

- **VITAMINS**

These are essential for us to function, and have to be sourced from food as we don't produce them by ourselves. They are necessary in order for us to function properly, stave off illness and grow to our greatest potential.

- **FAT-SOLUBLE VITAMINS**

These can be stored in our system, and released as needed. They include:

Vitamin A: Also known as Retinol, this builds the immune system and fights infections, and keeps skin and vision healthy.
SOURCES: *Whole milk, butter, egg yolks, liver, green vegetables, watercress, kale, spinach, prunes, carrots, squashes, sweet potatoes, oranges, apricots, peaches, melons and mangoes.*

Vitamin K: Responsible for blood clotting, wound healing and bone health.
SOURCES: *Spinach, kale, greens, broccoli, lettuce, watercress, cabbage, Brussels sprouts, liver, asparagus, oats, peas, green beans, butter, eggs, kelp.*

Vitamin D: Regulates the amount of calcium and phosphate in the body, keeping bones, teeth and the immune system healthy. It is very common for small children to be lacking in this vitamin, but a deficiency can lead to bone pain ('growing pains'), tenderness, bone deformities and rickets.
SOURCES: *SUNSHINE! Salmon, sardines, tuna, prawns, sunflower seeds, liver, eggs and mushrooms.*

Vitamin E: Acts as an antioxidant to protect cell membranes, and promotes a healthy immune system and growth.
SOURCES: *Wheatgerm oil, almonds, sesame oil, walnuts, cashews, pecans, sunflower seeds, sunflower oil, linseeds, olive oil, butter, spinach, salmon, brown rice, rye flour, pecans and carrots.*

- **WATER SOLUBLE VITAMINS**

If we consume an excess of these vitamins we excrete them via our kidneys. However, as they cannot be stored, a regular intake of them is required.

Vitamin Bs: These are eight water-soluble vitamins, including folic acid, which play a role in providing energy.
SOURCES: *Chickpeas, sunflower seeds, brown rice, fish, chicken, meat, clams, cashews, almonds, buckwheat, lentils, avocados, kale, rye, bananas, millet, oatmeal.*

Vitamin C: Protects cells, maintains connective tissue, helps wound healing.
SOURCES: *Sweet peppers, acerola cherries, kale, parsley, citrus fruits, watercress, strawberries, cabbage, asparagus, kiwis, broccoli, Brussels sprouts, melons and oysters.*

Folate: This is a B vitamin – the manmade version is called folic acid – which helps new tissues and proteins form, and aids digestion and nervous system development. It is crucial for pregnant women as it prevents birth defects.

SOURCES: *Yeast, black-eyed peas, liver, kidney beans, mung beans, lentils, walnuts, spinach, kale, cabbage, broccoli, peanuts, barley, almonds, oatmeal, figs and avocados.*

• MINERALS

Iron: Makes red blood cells to carry oxygen around the body for healthy growth, bone development, skin and nails.
SOURCES: *Kelp, yeast, molasses, pumpkin seeds, liver, sunflower seeds, millet, parsley, clams, almonds, cashews, prunes, red meat, raisins, chard, kale, dates, eggs, lentils, pulses, brown rice, dried apricots, dark/raw chocolate.*

Zinc: Antioxidant, anti-carcinogenic, anti-viral, wound-healing, aids reproductive health and growth and acts as a immune system regulator.
SOURCES: *Oysters, ginger, red meat, nuts, pulses, egg yolks, milk, chicken, sardines, buckwheat, prawns, oily fish, white fish.*

Magnesium: Helps turn food into energy, DNA repair, energy production and bone health.
SOURCES: *Seaweed, kelp, almonds, cashews, molasses, buckwheat, Brazil nuts, millet, tofu, coconut flesh, spinach, brown rice, dates, apricots, prawns, sweetcorn, avocados.*

Calcium: There is more of this in our bodies than any other mineral; it's crucial for children, building strong bones, teeth, nerve and muscle function, hormones and heartbeat regulation.
SOURCES: *Kelp, seaweed, dark leafy greens such as kale and spinach, cheese, almonds, parsley, sweetcorn, watercress, tofu, figs, sunflower seeds, buckwheat, sesame seeds, olives, broccoli.*

Manganese: Helps make and activate enzymes in the body, aids bone and ligament formation.
SOURCES: *Nuts, barley, buckwheat, split peas, wholemeal flour, spinach, oats, raisins, rhubarb, beans, avocados, Brussels sprouts.*

Potassium: Controls fluid balance, hormones, heart muscle and nerve function.
SOURCES: *Seaweed, red meat, chicken, potatoes, bananas, sunflower seeds, dates, figs, almonds, mushrooms, squash, carrots, yams, garlic, millet and pulses.*

Selenium: Antioxidant, reproductive health, DNA repair.
SOURCES: *Butter, Brazil nuts, cider vinegar, scallops, prawns, lobster, barley, oats, crab, chard, red meat, milk, fish, garlic, eggs, mushrooms, alfalfa.*

INDEX

This edition first published in Great Britain in 2017 by
Trapeze
an imprint of the Orion Publishing Group Ltd
Carmelite House
50 Victoria Embankment
London EC4Y 0DZ
An Hachette UK Company

1 3 5 7 9 10 8 6 4 2

A CIP catalogue record for this book is available
from the British Library.

ISBN: 978 1409 1 6703 7

Design: Nikki Dupin
Photography: Charlotte Kibbles
Food stylist: Natalie Thomson
Props stylist: Emma Lahaye
Illustrator: Kate Scally

Printed in Italy

www.orionbooks.co.uk

Nothing on these pages would exist without my husband, Robin; the calmest, kindest, happiest, smartest, most over-qualified plongeur, you are a rhyme with no riddle and I don't know how to begin to thank you.

My friends of old; Lili you have held me up always and added pizzazz to my punch with every breath. My first recipe tester then and always. Sascha for staying up late and talking when we can talk no more.

The best neighbours you could wish for, Ninfa and Panos; thank you for nightcaps, kitchen borrowing and baby napping when required!

To all who helped trial these recipes, particularly my transatlantic powerhouse of exuberance, detail and precision, Andi - I salute you. And the rest of the angels for love and support in spades, Erin, Gwen, Sarah, Susan and Tai.

My editor Anna, who came to me with a belief I didn't know I had and made this happen.

My agent Felicity, thank you for your calm, big-picture wisdom whenever I waivered. Char for oozing talent behind the lens. And Natalie for pimping my food so effortlessly.

All my friends who I've not seen for months! And those who've always been there to help: Zoe, Ren, Lex, Kerry, Lottie, Sarah, Natasha, Amy and Tommi.

To all of you who bought this book and read my blog, it's spurred me on and meant the world to me. Thank you.

My brother and sisters and amazing mum and dad; for all the food, the fun and the crazy, this wouldn't have happened otherwise.

But shining like beacons on a deep blue sea, my three lovely, smiling, sparkly children. Jethro, Calypso and Phoenix, above all, this is for you, for unwittingly pushing me, for tasting, devouring, guiding and (mostly!) adoring my food. My borderlines and open spaces. My absolute everything.